Home Health
Documentation

PROVEN STRATEGIES FOR CLINICIANS

Patricia A. Duclos-Miller, MS, RN, CNA, BC

Home Health Documentation: Proven Strategies for Clinicians is published by HCPro, Inc.

ISBN 978-1-60146-071-4

HCPro, Inc., provides information resources for the healthcare industry.

HCPro, Inc., is not affiliated in any way with The Joint Commission, which owns the JCAHO and Joint Commission trademarks.

Patricia A. Duclos-Miller, MS, RN, CNA, BC, Author
Elizabeth Petersen, Executive Editor
Emily Sheehan, Group Publisher
Sada Preisch, Proofreader
Susan Darbyshire, Art Director
Janell Lukac, Layout Artist
Anne Kilgore, Layout Artist
Darren Kelly, Books Production Supervisor
Claire Cloutier, Production Manager
Jean St. Pierre, Director of Operations

Advice given is general. Readers should consult professional counsel for specific legal, ethical, or clinical questions.

Arrangements can be made for quantity discounts. For more information, contact:

HCPro, Inc.
P.O. Box 1168
Marblehead, MA 01945
Telephone: 800/650-6787 or 781/639-1872
Fax: 781/639-2982
E-mail: *customerservice@hcpro.com*

Visit HCPro at its World Wide Web sites:
www.hcpro.com and *www.hcmarketplace.com*

Contents

About the author vi

Dedication vii

Acknowledgement vii

Chapter 1: Key aspects of documentation 1
What every nurse case manager needs to know 1
Clinical supervisor responsibilities 4
Let the nursing process be your guide 5
Organizational policies, protocols, and practices 18
Documentation of what was taught 20

Chapter 2: Reducing risk and culpability through defensive documentation 23
Your documentation: Truth or consequences? 23
Legal risks with IV therapy 27
Legal risks in skin care 28
Handling documentation errors 30
Adverse events: When bad things happen to good nurses 31
Incident reports 35
Risk-reduction strategies 37

Chapter 3: Contemporary nursing practice 41
Are you using contemporary nursing practice? 41
Certification 43
Professional standards 46
Code of ethics 49
State Nurse Practice Act 50
Threats to licensure 52
Professional boundaries in home care 53
Federal and state regulations 54
The Joint Commission 56
CHAP accreditation 57
Organizational policies and procedures 57
Competency assessment 59
Disease management in home healthcare 60

Chapter 4: Clinical documentation 65

The effects of staff documentation on compliance, quality, and reimbursement......................... 65

Clinical record as communication.. 66

Clinical record as a demonstration of compliance 67

PRO and managed-care standards.. 69

The Joint Commission and 'tracer methodology'... 70

Quality and risk-management review 73

Clinical record as a path to reimbursement.. 75

Clinical record and pay for performance 78

Chapter 5: Nursing negligence: Understanding your risks and culpability 81

Legal issues 81

Essential definitions... 81

Factors that contribute to malpractice cases against nurses 83

Home healthcare litigation... 85

Wound care negligence... 86

Averting legal issues about falls 87

Averting legal issues with IV therapy 88

Legal risks for clinical managers 90

Negligent supervision... 91

Imputed liability 91

Manage your risk.. 91

Legal risks for nurses.. 93

Professional-negligence claims against nurses... 94

National Practitioner Data Bank 94

Chapter 6: Improving your documentation.. 99

Recognizing and correcting charting mistakes that increase your liability risks 99

Eight common charting errors 100

The consequences of an incomplete clinical record... 104

Tips to improve your documentation 105

Chapter 7: Developing a foolproof documentation system 111

Building on the foundation of compliance standards... 111

Evaluating your current documentation system 112

Systems of documentation.. 113

Using the Joint Commission standards as the foundation of your system............................. 123

Ten steps for ensuring a foolproof documentation system.. 129

Chapter 8: Auditing your documentation system 133

The important role audits play in protecting you and your organization 133

Building your audit system around performance improvement goals 133

Measuring compliance and improvement through an audit 135

Getting your staff to use the audit tool 136

Advantages of audits for the clinical supervisor 137

Clinical supervisor tips for auditing 138

Chapter 9: Telehealth and electronic health records in home care 139

Introduction 139

How to build a computerized system that reduces liability 140

Why we need EHRs 141

Start at the beginning 143

Benefits of electronic documentation 144

The clinical supervisor's role 146

Challenges associated with change 147

Computer etiquette 148

The dos and don'ts of developing an electronic documentation system 149

Strategies for success 150

Legal risks with telehealth in home healthcare 152

Chapter 10: Motivating yourself and others to document completely and accurately ... 155

Why nurses document poorly 155

Change: Embrace it or resist it 157

The role of education and expectations 159

The good, the bad, and the ugly approach 160

Monitoring the work environment 161

Appendix 165

About the author

Patricia A. Duclos-Miller, MS, RN, CNA, BC

Patricia A. Duclos-Miller, MS, RN, CNA, BC is currently a full-time associate professor in nursing at Capital Community College in Hartford, CT. In addition to this position, she is a senior consultant for the Kelsco Consulting Group in Cheshire, CT; a special lecturer for the University of Connecticut's management in nursing graduate program; and a clinical QI analyst at Bristol Hospital, CT.

Duclos-Miller is a registered nurse, board certified by the American Nurses Credentialing Center (ANCC) in nursing administration. During her 33 years in nursing, she has been a director for quality improvement; director of nursing in acute, home health, and long-term care settings; and a staff nurse in the specialties of medical-surgical, mother-baby, and neonatal intensive care nursing. She is a recognized speaker on contemporary nursing topics, including quality improvement, team building, and documentation issues.

Duclos-Miller has served in key leadership positions for professional nursing organizations and is a contributor to the newsletter **Strategies for Nurse Managers**, published by HCPro, Inc. She is the author of *Stressed Out About Your First Year of Nursing,* the first and second editions of *Managing Documentation Risk: A Guide for Nurse Managers,* and the first and second editions of the handbook *Nursing Documentation: Reduce Your Risk of Liability,* all published by HCPro, Inc.

Dedication

To my loving family, Wayne, Matthew, and Nathan. They continue to support me in every endeavor.

Acknowledgement

I would like to thank everyone who took time out of their very busy schedules to talk with me about this topic. Everyone was honest an helpful. They assured me that I had captured the reality of nursing documentation in home health care. Thank you to Chellon Wilkinson, Sr. Jean MgGinty, Carol Ann Thoman, Diana McKenna, Bristol Hospital home care nurses, and Regina McNamara.

Key aspects of documentation

Learning objectives

After reading this chapter, the participant will be able to:

- Identify why documentation is important in the home health care setting
- Discuss how the nursing process is used in nursing documentation
- Describe how to use Nursing Outcomes Classification (NOC) in nursing documentation

What every nurse case manager needs to know

In home health care today, every member of the team is accountable for factual, accurate, complete and timely documentation. However, the nurse case manager is really the focus of any clinical record review. In today's culture of quality and accountability, your role and scope of responsibilities, as demonstrated by your documentation, will bring you under scrutiny. Your documentation reveals your commitment to quality patient care. As the case manager you must recognize the importance of good clinical documentation. It is also vital that you assist everyone working on your case to practice defensive documentation and avoid the potential for legal consequences if a case is reviewed for alleged malpractice, substandard care, or fraudulent practices. According to Newfield, "Through effective communication, documentation, and post-incident procedures, proper care may be defended and unnecessary exposure avoided" (2006).

Focusing on "better rather than more" with respect to documentation is a good axiom to remember. The clinical record must be accurate and complete but does not need to be overwhelming. The information it contains is crucial for a number of people and functions. It is used to communicate patients' progress to other clinical and nonclinical staff. It is also used by the agency's quality and risk-management department. In all cases, the accuracy and completeness of the clinical record is essential for reimbursement from payers. If there is a question of the care that was given, it is also used by an auditor to determine substandard professional care, which may also be considered negligent. And if your agency is accredited by CHAP (Community Health Accreditation Program) or The Joint Commission, the clinical record, as well as on-site visits, is used to measure compliance with accreditation standards.

Documenting completely and accurately is considered a professional standard of nursing practice. Documentation demonstrates the quality of care given, establishes reimbursement entitlement, and substantiates the need for services (Mahler, 2001). For every step in the nursing process, the care delivered must be documented. Whether you are a clinical supervisor assisting your staff or a case manager, it is every nurse's responsibility to fulfill the necessary requirements of good clinical care and documentation. Doing so not only validates the universally recognized professional approach to patient care, it supplies other care providers with consistent, clear communication and validates critical decision-making that is often necessary for quality patient care.

There are many research studies that have attempted to identify why nurses do not value the importance of their documentation. And in one study Moody and Snyder found an estimated 15–20% of the nursing work time is spent in documentation. Although documentation may not be valued by nurses it is still a requirement, regardless of the work setting. In today's climate of accountability and service expectations it is more critical now than in past years. We know that documentation has changed over the last few decades in both its appearance and the advent of new technology in an attempt to facilitate data entry and access. What is still missing with these changes is the failure to demonstrate patient continuity of care and the evaluation of patient outcomes (Irving et al. 2006).

The quality of the care provided to patients can only be measured by the quality of the nursing documentation. The major reasons for documenting nursing care include:

- Documentation of the assessment
- Documentation of the plan of care
- Coordination of services provided
- Evaluation of the effectiveness of the care provided
- Facilitation of communication with other providers
- Reimbursement for services provided

According to Marrelli, the importance of the home care clinical record relates to the fact that the clinical record is:

1. The only written source for communication among the home care team members
2. The written source that supports insurance payment
3. The written evidence of clinical decision-making
4. The legal record of client care

5. The basis for evaluation of care provided by peers; auditors; licensing, accreditation, and government surveyor review

6. The evidence that demonstrates meeting the professional standard of care (Marelli, 2001)

Failure to document completely can have legal consequences. If documentation is incomplete, contains gaps, or is not consistently completed according to the organization's policies, it can be used to support an allegation that negligent care was provided. Even worse, documentation of care or services provided when in fact they did not occur is open to "failure-of-care" accusation. These failure-of-care cases are initiated by the government when the healthcare provider submits bills for grossly substandard care that are equal to no care at all (Hess, 2005).

Incomplete documentation allows for juries or surveyors to conclude that the nurse did not collect sufficient data and plan appropriate care; implement appropriate interventions, according to professional and agency standards; make good clinical decisions; and communicate effectively. A Medicare survey citation frequently results when:

- Documentation does not support that the plan of care was coordinated, or

- Services delivered are not exactly those ordered in the plan of care" (Hollers, 2004)

According to Marrelli, there are five areas that have increased in importance of clinical documentation.

Factors contributing to importance of documentation	Reality check (or today's expectation)
Emphasis on value and cost	- Third-party payers have increased their scrutiny and control of resources - Documentation must demonstrate skilled care was provided - Pay for performance will be in home health care
Emphasis on quality improvement	- Patient outcomes are now indicators of quality care - Documentation must demonstrate care and achievement of stated goals - Documentation needs to demonstrate care coordination and collaboration - Timely returns of the 485 and MD orders - Competency assessment of the staff - OASIS used for demonstrating quality care based on outcomes

Factors contributing to importance of documentation	Reality check (or today's expectation)
Emphasis on standards of care and processes	• Defined levels of care based on evidence-based practices • Use of clinical practice guidelines or clinical paths • Government has developed clinical practice guidelines to move to a standardization in healthcare (see *www.guideline.gov*) • Patient/caregiver and payer satisfaction critical to agency's survival
Emphasis on capturing fraud and abuse	• Clinical documentation must be F-A-C-T (factual, accurate, complete, and timely)
Emphasis on effectiveness and efficiency	• Automation to help prevent duplication of clinical and administrative information • Quality versus quantity in documentation • Effective documentation supports appropriate care

(Marrelli, 2001)

Clinical supervisor responsibilities

As a member of the management team, it is your responsibility to assist your staff in adhering to both clinical and documentation standards. It is also your responsibility to provide continuing education, professional feedback, and input into policy and documentation-system changes whenever possible. It is to your advantage to fulfill these responsibilities because if your staff is involved in a government audit or survey, your ability to manage and meet quality and risk-management standards will be called into question.

In home health care the clinical supervisor must not only demonstrate a commitment to providing safe and efficient patient care, but also ensure that every clinical record reflects that commitment. That is, although you must ensure that nursing staff comply with up-to-date standards, it is equally important to ensure that they document that compliance accurately and completely.

Your role is to support an efficient and effective documentation system and to create an expectation that the system be followed. It is also your responsibility to ensure competent and contemporary care is being given to the clients. The nurse case managers must have excellent assessment and documentation skills. The assessment skills are needed for reimbursement, and the documentation of that comprehensive assessment within the defined time frames determines the reimbursement (Marrelli, 2001).

Nursing management can demonstrate support for such a system by:

- Developing an efficient system that meets the requirements of regulatory standards.

- Involving the end users in the development of the system.

- Emphasizing the importance of documentation through routine audits, written guidelines, policies, job descriptions, and performance appraisals. The language should include stipulations for daily supervisory oversight, audits of the system, and feedback to the staff.

Let the nursing process be your guide

The nursing process, as outlined by the American Nurses Association's (ANA's) *Nursing Scope and Standards of Practice*, provides us with an established, scientific approach to providing nursing care. Not only does each step guide us in our approach, it tells us how to validate what we saw, heard, felt, smelled, said, and did while providing that care. The process accounts for all significant data and actions taken by a registered nurse, the documentation of which is used for critical decision-making. Therefore, your documentation of patient care should follow the framework of the nursing process.

Assessment

The first step of the nursing process is assessment. In this step, the nurse collects information about the patient's condition, which could include the patient's history, the physical exam, laboratory data, and so on. So as not to become overwhelmed, the nurse must decide which information is most useful to the care of the patient. For example, a nurse could limit the assessment data to the admission signs and symptoms, the chief complaint, or medical diagnosis. This first step in the nursing process—assessment—should always be evident in the medical record as it provides a complete clinical picture of the patient. In home health care the OASIS is an integral piece of an agency's clinical documentation system. The nurse must understand the importance of data collection and its long-term impact on home care. Your critical thinking skills are self-evident when you are able to combine all assessment data and the OASIS items, which then provide a complete picture of the patient and his or her care needs. According to Pentz and Wilson credibility and critical thinking are two major sources of inaccurate data collection (Yadgood et al., 2005).

An assessment should include both subjective and objective data. When documenting this data, beware of inappropriate documentation practices and focus on quality and risk management strategies.

Subjective data

In this context, subjective data are data that can be observed, but not measured. Statements made by the patient or family/significant other are examples of subjective data. Although every conversation may not be relevant to the interaction, there will be times when a patient's words need to be recorded to establish a clear picture of how the patient perceives his or her status.

For instance, if the patient says something that can be used to demonstrate mental, behavioral, or cognitive status at the time of the assessment, documentation of the conversation can be used to measure progress or decline over the course of treatment. If patients are unable to speak or are cognitively impaired, nonverbal cues are essential in determining whether there has been any change in status.

These conversations with the patient/family will need to be captured in the clinical record in order to provide other clinicians with an accurate depiction of the patient's current status.

Objective data

Nurses establish patients' clinical status based on objective data, which are observable and measurable. Physical exams of patients, which include key assessment techniques such as inspection, palpation, percussion, and auscultation, provide objective data about patients' health status. In simpler terms, nurses' objective assessments are based on what is seen, heard, felt, and smelt. Healthcare providers find this much easier to validate and include in their documentation than subjective data. Objective data also includes the results of diagnostic tests.

When recording this data, however, there are risks your staff should consider. If the objective data is not reviewed in a timely manner, a reviewer of the clinical record may point out that you failed to interpret the data and address significant changes of condition. There also may be situations in which critical objective data were present but there was no subsequent documentation of an appropriate intervention. In addition, if the absence of critical objective data resulted in a gap in the clinical picture of the patient, it may contribute to a lack of appropriate intervention identification. All of these situations can lead to quality and risk-management issues.

Good nursing documentation should tell a story about the client and their problems. Just like when reading a book, the reader can understand the story. There is a beginning, middle, and end. The nurse must document every visit in a way that supports moving the client to the stated outcomes on the 485. Documentation also includes the client's homebound, admission, or general assessment status as well as the skill provided at that visit. "Focus is on the patient's problems in the documentation and why home care is involved; and, from any payer's perspective is what they must see to authorize payment" (Marrelli, 2001).

Practical tips

Remember that the OASIS data elements are the basis for appropriate reimbursement and demonstrate client outcomes:

- Resolve client problems in a timely manner
- Support the client's homebound status in functional terms
- Review your own charting and ask yourself if someone else would know "why" the client is homebound and if the care is moving the client to the stated goals

(Marrelli, 2001)

Gaps in documentation on any clinical assessment tool leave the nurse and the agency open to allegations that they failed to document assessments or failed to address significant changes of condition. For example, in the case of an incomplete assessment of I&O, it could be alleged that the lack of analysis, intervention, and accurate documentation was the cause of circulatory collapse, dehydration, renal failure, infections, skin breakdown, or even death.

For the nurse to arrive at a nursing diagnosis and the development of a nursing plan of care, the assessment findings are crucial. Be sure you are completing all assessment tools thoroughly.

Here are some risk management tips for documenting assessment findings:

- Describe everything exactly as found by inspection, palpation, percussion, or auscultation
- Do not allow the use of general terms such as "normal," "abnormal," "good," or "poor"
- Be specific, and include both negative and positive aspects
- Adhere to your policies' time frames on completion of assessments
- Document your assessment as soon as possible after completing it

Nursing diagnosis and Nursing Outcome Classification

If nurses accurately perform the assessment process, they will be able to appropriately establish nursing diagnoses. This phase of the nursing process demonstrates that the nurse reviewed the appropriate data available at the time and made a professional determination of the clinical problem(s) at that time. Once the nurse makes a clinical nursing diagnosis based on a thorough assessment, the rest of the process falls into place.

The nursing diagnosis is defined by the North American Nursing Diagnosis Association International (NANDA International) as a "clinical judgment about the individual, family, or community responses to actual and potential health problems/life processes. Nursing diagnoses provide the basis for selection of nursing interventions to achieve outcomes for which the nurse is accountable" (Doenges, 2006). Therefore, the nursing diagnosis expresses the nurse's professional judgment of the patient's clinical status, the anticipated response to treatment, and the potential nursing-care needs. It guides the nurse and subsequent providers in their understanding of the patient's problem(s) and the plan of care developed specifically for that problem(s).

If your agency chooses to include the nursing diagnosis in its documentation system, you should promote consistency and use of correct terminology by adopting NANDA International terminology. The NANDA International diagnostic headings, coupled with the patient's clinical etiology, provide a clear picture of the patient's needs.

Risk for falls

NANDA definition: Increased susceptibility to falling that may cause physical harm

Examples of general risk factors
History of falls; wheelchair use; 65 years of age or older; lives alone; lower limb prosthesis; use of assistive devices

Physiological risk factors
Presence of acute illness; visual difficulties; hearing difficulties; arthritis; orthostatic hypotension; sleeplessness; anemia; decreased lower extremity strength; postprandial blood sugar changes, etc.

Medication risk factors
Antihypertensive agents; ACE inhibitors; diuretics; tricyclic antidepressants; alcohol use; antianxiety agents; opiates; hypnotics or tranquilizers

Environmental risk factors
Weather conditions such as wet floors/ice; scatter rugs; clutter, etc.

(Ladwig, 2006)

History of nursing outcomes

The use of patient outcomes in documentation dates back to the mid-1960s, when for the first time nursing outcomes were used to evaluate the effectiveness of nursing care. The use of patient outcomes to evaluate healthcare dates back to Florence Nightingale, who recorded and analyzed healthcare conditions and the subsequent outcomes of those conditions during the Crimean War (Moorhead et al., 2004).

Although nurses have documented outcomes of their nursing interventions for decades, there was no common language or associated way to measure the outcomes of these interventions in the past. Today, however, a research team at the University of Iowa has given nursing a standardized terminology for nursing-specific and nursing-sensitive outcomes. This comprehensive classification of nursing outcomes is called the Nursing Outcomes Classification (NOC).

The current 2004 NOC lists 330 outcomes for use in nursing documentation. Each NOC nursing outcome has a predetermined definition, a measurement scale, and associated interventions. Each describes a possible state, behavior, or perception of the patient (this is different from nursing diagnosis, which describes a patient's problem, either actual or potential). Once the nursing diagnosis is made, the nurse seeks to resolve it through appropriate interventions (see an example in Figure 1.1).

Figure 1.1 Knowledge: Disease Process (1803)

Domain—Health Knowledge and Behavior
Class—Health Knowledge
Scale(s)—None to Extensive (i)

Indicators		None 1	Limited 2	Moderate 3	Substantial 4	Extensive 5
180302	Description of specific disease process	1	2	3	4	5
180303	Description of cause or contributing factors	1	2	3	4	5
180304	Description of risk factors	1	2	3	4	5
180305	Description of effects of disease	1	2	3	4	5
180306	Description of signs and symptoms	1	2	3	4	5
180307	Description of usual disease course	1	2	3	4	5
180308	Description of measures to minimize disease progression	1	2	3	4	5
180309	Description of complications	1	2	3	4	5
180310	Description of signs and symptoms of complications	1	2	3	4	5
180311	Description of precautions to prevent complications	1	2	3	4	
Specify disease:						

1st edition 1997; Revised 3rd edition

Reprinted from *Iowa Outcomes Project Nursing Outcomes Classification (NOC)*, 3rd edition, page 352. Copyright 2004 with permission from Elsevier.

Or you could simply state your outcomes as:

- The patient will explain the disease state, recognize the need for medications, and understand treatments (and just add the end date of the 60-day plan)

- The patient will demonstrate how to perform health-related procedures satisfactorily by _____ (Ladwig, 2006)

Nursing Outcomes Classification, 3rd edition, cited those nursing diagnoses and NOC outcomes home care nurses selected.

NOC outcomes selected for NANDA diagnoses for home care patients	
NANDA diagnoses	Possible NOC outcomes to use
Knowledge deficit	Knowledge: Diet Knowledge: Disease process Knowledge: Energy conservation Knowledge: Health resources Knowledge: Infection control Knowledge: Medication Knowledge: Prescribed activity Knowledge: Treatment procedures Knowledge: Treatment regimen Self-Care: Nonparenteral medication Self-Care: Parenteral medication
Caregiver role strain	Caregiver home care readiness Caregiver lifestyle disruption Caregiver-patient relationship Caregiver physical health Caregiver performance: Direct care Caregiver Performance: Indirect care Caregiver well-being

(Moorhead, 2004)

Core outcomes were also selected by nursing organizations representing specialty practices such as home healthcare. According to the Home Healthcare Nurses Association the following core outcomes.

Comfort level	Knowledge: Disease Process
Community risk control: Communicable disease	Knowledge: Illness Care
Health beliefs	Knowledge: Medication
Health beliefs: Perceived ability to perform	Knowledge: Prescribed activity
Health beliefs: Perceived control	Knowledge: Treatment regimen
Health beliefs: Perceived resources	Medication Response
Health beliefs: Perceived threat	Treatment behavior: Illness or injury
Health orientation	Self-care: Nonparenteral medication
	Wound healing: Secondary intention

(Moorhead, 2004)

In using the NOC outcomes you are demonstrating evidence-based nursing practice with quantitative data to support the effects of your nursing actions and progress in the plan of care. Many of the NOC outcomes are "reliable and valid for use in documenting the effectiveness of nursing interventions" (Moorhead, 2004).

A good example of the integration and use of outcomes identification can be found in home healthcare. The Centers for Medicare & Medicaid Services (CMS) requires all Medicare-certified home health organizations to use the OASIS data set, which they have been doing since 1998. The OASIS outcomes system contains core measures that have been identified as applicable to all client groups. It also contains measures specific to client groups with a particular diagnosis or problem, the outcomes of which are measured on scales specific to them. Using the OASIS outcome system, nurses assess whether home health clients have improved, stabilized, or deteriorated (Sparks and Taylor, 2001).

Outcomes identification

If you do not elect to use the NOC outcomes then the next step in the nursing process is to determine an expected outcome, or goal, for the patient. The outcome must be derived from the nursing diagnosis and documented as a measurable, realistic, and patient-focused goal. It must include a target time or date as well as an objective measurable action that the patient is expected to achieve.

Whenever possible, include the patient/family's perspective on the goal of treatment and the time frame. The expected outcomes also should reflect the continuum of care, from admission, addressing immediate and intermediate outcomes, for planning for discharge and follow-up care.

Tips for documenting expected outcomes

1. Be specific
2. Be realistic
3. It must be measurable
4. Define the time frame for achieving the outcome
5. Include the patient/family's desires and resources

(Doenges, 2006)

Goal setting is stated in the locator 22 on the CMS 485. Usually the goals are stated in generic terms. The best way to write goals is to think about your expectations about the outcomes and write them according to the tips above.

EXAMPLE of GENERIC:

"All body systems will return to WNL"

"Client will not have any urinary incontinence"

OUTCOME BASED:

"Client will regain independence in dressing upper body"

"Client will be able to control urinary incontinence through timed voiding" (Hollers, 2004)

Planning

The next step in the nursing process is to develop a plan of care for the patient based on the nurse's assessment/diagnosis. Documentation of this phase demonstrates that the clinical status of the patient was recognized and that the nurse then developed an appropriate plan of care. It shows that the nursing process was in place and thereby decreases the risk of incomplete or incorrect care. Having a written "road map" helps everyone involved provide safe and quality care.

When developing a plan of care use the following guidelines:

- Review identified nursing diagnoses and rank them in order of priority
- Use evidence-based nursing interventions or clinical guidelines/pathways
- Include nursing diagnosis, expected outcomes, nursing interventions, and evaluation of care
- The plan of care should be used as a communication tool between all home care team members and the client (Sparks and Taylor, 2001)

This step of the nursing process can be documented in a variety of ways. You can use a specially designed form, flow sheet, 485, daily visit notes, nursing progress notes, clinical pathway, or specific software module. But whatever format is used, remember that the patient plan of care is a permanent part of the clinical record and is used to evaluate the care that was provided. Adjustments to the plan of care should reflect a progression of care based on the client's needs.

Medicare care planning	
Qualifying service	**Key components of documentation**
Skilled observation and assessment	Findings and judgments Contacts with physician when indicated In-depth assessment of issues or body systems relevant to patient's medical instability
Client education	Comprehension level Subject matter taught Response to the teaching Knowledge and skills acquired
Therapy services	Performance of treatments based on MD orders Response to treatment Any efforts to locate caregivers who can learn to safely and appropriately perform treatments Communication with MD of any evidence of ineffective treatment
Management and evaluation of a complex plan of care	Interventions and evaluations showing management of the plan Successes and failures Modifications made Patient/caregiver satisfaction and condition Capability and endurance of the caregivers Contribution of other professionals

(Hollers, 2004)

What to write in a home healthcare patient's plan of care can be a difficult task for the case manager. We are bound by the Medicare CoPs and must follow their directives. According to the Medicare CoPs, "the POC must contain all pertinent diagnoses, including:

- The patient's mental status;

- The types of services, supplies, and equipment required;

- The frequency of the visits to be made;

- Prognosis;

- Rehabilitation potential;

- Functional limitations;

- Activities permitted;

- Nutritional requirements;

- All medications and treatments;

- Safety measures to protect against injury;

- Instructions for timely discharge or referral; and

- Any additional items the HHA or physician choose to include."
  (CMS Publication 100-2, Chapter 7, Section 30.2.1)

Unfortunately, one of the most commonly cited deficiencies in home healthcare is the failure to follow the plan of care. Be sure that you have a thorough assessment to begin the process. Then decide the critical nursing interventions and measurable outcomes. Some agencies have software to help the case managers. The OASIS data is integrated into the plan of care (485). However, it still requires the case manager to analyze the assessment data and determine the pertinent diagnoses and the development of a realistic plan of care.

Out of the top 10 state deficiencies cited for home health agencies in Arizona for fiscal year 2006–2007, three related to the adherence to the plan of care:

- Home health services shall be provided by the home health agency in accordance with a written plan of care established and authorized by a physician

- The plan of care shall be based on the patient's diagnoses and the assessment of the patient's immediate and long-term needs

- The plan of care shall include the following: Treatments, medications, and any drug allergies; and type and frequency of services to be provided (Arizona Dept. of Health Services, 2007)

Stoker reported the top 10 deficiencies cited for home health agencies nationwide in 2004, including plan of care and examples of the need for good nursing documentation:

1. Plan of care was not established or reviewed

2. Plan of care did not cover patient diagnoses, services, or visits

3. The clinical record was incomplete as it failed to include findings

4. Assessments did not include medication review

5. The clinicians did not notify the MD to significant changes in the patient's condition

6. Drugs and prescriptions were not given as ordered

7. The HHAide supervisory visits were not conducted as needed

8. There was no evidence of coordination of services

9. The clinical record did not identify coordination of services

10. The case manager (RN) did not routinely reevaluate the patient care needs. (Stoker, 2005)

Implementation

Based on the nursing plan of care and contemporary standards of nursing care, the nurse then documents the care provided for the patient. This phase of the nursing process includes working collaboratively with other members of the healthcare team, the patient, and the patient's family. Implementation may include some of the following interventions:

- Assessing and monitoring

- Therapeutic interventions

- Comfort measures

- Assistance with activities of daily living

- Supporting respiratory functions

- Supporting elimination functions

- Providing skin care

- Managing the environment to promote a therapeutic milieu

- Providing food and fluids

- Giving emotional support

- Teaching and/or counseling

- Referral to other agencies or services (Sparks and Taylor, 2001)

Documentation will need to include the specific nurse's intervention and the patient's response to the intervention. It should reflect the coordination of care, health teaching and promotion, and any consultation that was done on behalf of the patient. Like the documentation of planning, the documentation of care provided can be assigned to a specific form or location in the clinical record.

Evaluation

In this step of the nursing process, the nurse reviews the progress made in achieving established outcomes. The documentation needed to validate this step includes the nurse's comments on whether his or her assessment, diagnosis, achievement of outcomes, plan of care, and nursing interventions were successful. In addition, when developing a documentation system or a continuing education program for nurses, ensure that each nurse assesses the effectiveness of the nursing process.

In determining whether the patient received high-quality care the nurse must document the patient's response to care, the patient's compliance with prescribed medications and therapies, the progress being made toward the stated goal, and the caregiver's ability to learn and resume all or part of the treatment plan (Hollers, 2004).

If the nurse uses the evaluation phase properly, the documentation will reflect high-quality nursing care.

Figure 1.2 shows the flow of the process and identifies the tools associated with each phase.

Figure 1.2 Nursing process flow chart

Assessment

Definition: Subjective and objective data from patient's health history, physical examination, medical record, diagnostic test results

Tools: Physical-assessment form
Nursing admission assessment
OASIS
Diagnostic test results forms
Computer software module

Nursing Diagnosis

Definition: Clinical nursing judgment based on the assessment data

Tools: Plan of care (485)
Patient-care guidelines
Clinical pathways
Medication reconciliation record
Progress notes
Problem list
Computer software module

Outcome Identification

Definition: Specific measurable outcome

Tools: Nursing Outcome Classification (NOC)
Plan of care
Clinical pathway
Computer software module
Federally mandated documentation systems

Planning

Definition: Establish care priorities, set measurable goals/outcomes with target dates, describe interventions

Tools: Plan of care (485)
Patient care guidelines
Clinical pathway
Discharge plan/summary
Computer software module

Implementation

Definition: Actual nursing interventions delivered

Tools: Skilled visit flow sheets
Progress notes
Computer software module

Evaluation

Definition: Reassess data, nursing diagnoses, and interventions for achievement of stated outcome

Tools: Skilled visit flow sheets
Clinical pathway
Computer software module

Organizational policies, protocols, and practices

When nurse experts are asked to review a medical record in preparation for a legal case, they rely heavily on the clinical record to determine the following:

- Did the healthcare provider meet the policies and protocols of the organization at the time of the care?

- More importantly, did the healthcare provider meet the standards of nursing practice at the time of the care?

It is therefore the responsibility of the nursing management team and the nursing staff to follow the established policies of the organization and that this compliance is demonstrated in the documentation system for that organization.

Organizational policies, protocols, and practices will always be called into review when there is an allegation of substandard patient care. Nursing practice will be held to national and local professional nursing standards, which are available through the ANA and through specialty nursing associations. If you derive your policies and procedures from these, your organization will be better able to justify that the care that was delivered met established professional standards.

In the cognitive section of the patient care flow sheet, the notations indicated, "No changes in mental status, no decreased level of consciousness, disorientation, or confusion."

In the narrative notes, the nurse notes, "Skin cool, clammy, no peripheral edema, ashen in color. No cyanosis noted."

Case study

Good documentation reflects the nursing process

Scenario: A patient complains of chest pain. The nurse takes the patient seriously, as the subjective complaint may indicate a myocardial infarction. He or she acts quickly, performing a focused assessment and documenting the essential information. Here are the critical elements of good documentation of a patient with chest pain.

Documentation of what the patient said: Subjective data

7/15/07 1600

Patient stated, "Nurse, I am having chest pain." See pain flow sheet for description, location, intensity noted. Patient in chair, increasingly anxious. Used calm, reassuring behavior with patient. Redirected her to focus on remaining calm for interventions to work. Patient responded, and pulse and respirations decreased. See VS section of flow sheet.

The patient's exact description of the symptom was noted, and the nurse used quotations around the patient's words, rather than recording his or her interpretation of them.

On the pain flow sheet, the nurse indicates *pain was located in the substernal region, radiating to the left shoulder. Pain level 10 out of 10.* The nurse appropriately uses the pain scale to measure the level of intensity.

The nurse also notes on the pain flow sheet: *No preceding activity or past history of this type of pain. Steady pain: 2–3 minutes. No SOB.*

Patient care flow sheet indicated that the initial pulse and respirations at the time of the nurse's initial assessment of pain were:

7/15/07 1600 P: 120 R: 40 BP: 146/90
7/15/07 1604 P: 96 R: 28 BP: 124/85

Documentation of what was assessed: Objective data

In the cardiopulmonary section of the patient care flow sheet, the nurse writes

AR. Irregular regular rhythm. No JVD. O2 sats on RA: 92%. Color ashen, skin cool and clammy.

The nurse documents the vital signs, noting tachycardia, an increased respiratory rate, and above-baseline blood pressure for this patient. In addition, the nurse records auscultation of heart sounds (e.g., regular/irregular heart rate, murmur, gallops, rubs.)

The nurse assesses lung sounds and the respiratory rate and pattern, and measures abnormal O2 saturation via pulse oximetry. The patient's actions are already noted as increasingly anxious. There is no clutching of the chest by the patient. Skin assessment also is conducted and documented.

In the cognitive section of the patient care flow sheet, the notations indicated:

Case study

Good documentation reflects the nursing process (cont.)

No changes in mental status; no decreased level of consciousness, disorientation, or confusion.

In the narrative notes, the nurse notes: Skin cool, clammy, no peripheral edema, ashen in color. No cyanosis noted.

Documentation of what was done: Intervention

The nurse continues to document his or her interventions and the patient's responses.

Frequent monitoring: The VSs were noted every few minutes until the chest pain subsided. 911 was called. All treatment activities are documented, including medications administered, such as aspirin and/or nitroglycerin.

Oxygen therapy: The nurse documents the patient's initial pulse-oximetry reading, respiratory-assessment findings.

The pulse-oximetry assessments are documented until within normal range or transferred to emergency personnel.

Cardiac monitoring: 7/15/07 1615 Patient placed on cardiac monitor by EMS. Patient informed as to the reason for continuous monitoring.

The nurse does document notification of the physician of the patient's change of condition and transfer to the hospital. He or she records the physician's response and his or her actions.

Communication: The nurse is good at documenting his or her communication with other healthcare team members. It is found in his or her narrative notes, names, time of notification, etc.

Emotional support: 7/15/07 16200 Patient increasing in anxiety; reassurance given and questions answered.

Transfer to hospital: This patient needed to be transferred, and the nurse documented the aspects of the patient's condition that warranted the transfer. The report to the physician was documented. The nurse also would have recorded the name of the person who accompanied the patient and which monitoring devices were in place during the transport.

Documentation of what was taught

The teaching plan needs to be tailored to the patient's condition and treatment. Documentation of patient/family teaching needs to include what was taught, the method of teaching, the materials used for teaching, how well the patient/family understood the teaching, etc.

Resources

www.guideline.gov National Guideline Clearinghouse (NGC), a public resource for evidence-based clinical practice guidelines.

References

Doenges, M. 2006. *Nursing Care Plans Guidelines for Individualizing Client Care Across the Life Span.* Philadelphia: F. A. Davis.

Goldberg, K. 1999. *Surefire Documentation: How, What, and When Nurses Need to Document.* Philadelphia: Mosby.

Hess, C. 2005. "The art of skin and wound care documentation." *Home Health Nurse* 23(8):502–513.

Hollers, K. 2004. "Using the nursing process to accurately plan the Medicare 60-day episode of care." *Home Health Nurse* 22(1):28–33.

Irving, K., et al. 2006. "Discursive practices in the documentation of patient assessments." *Journal of Advanced Nursing* 53(2):151–159.

Ladwig, G. 2006. *Mosby's Guide to Nursing Diagnosis.* St. Louis: Mosby Elsevier.

Mahler, C. 2001. "Just the Facts, Please: A Guide to Effective Documentation." *Home Care Provider* 6(4):120–125.

Marrelli, T. 2001. *Handbook of Home Health Standards and Documentation Guidelines for Reimbursement.* Philadelphia: Mosby.

Medicare Benefit Policy Manual, CMS. 2005. Chapter 7: Home Health Services. Accessed July 11, 2007, from *www.cms.hhs.gov/manuals/Downloads/bp102c07.pdf.*

Moorhead, S., et al. 2004. *Iowa Outcomes Project Nursing Outcomes Classification (NOC),* 3rd edition. St. Louis: Mosby.

Newfield, J. S. 2006. "Documentation: Focusing on better rather than more." *Home Health Care Management and Practice* 18(3):247–249.

Sparks, S., and C. Taylor. 2001. *Nursing Diagnosis Reference Manual,* 5th edition. Springhouse, PA: Springhouse.

Stoker, J. 2005. "Legislative regulatory update: CMS updates on surveys and payment policy." *Home Healthcare Nurse* 23(7):470.

Yadgood, M., et al. 2005. "Solving the mystery: The role of competency assessment in OASIS documentation" *Home Healthcare Nurse* 23(4):224–231.

Reducing risk and culpability through defensive documentation

Learning objectives

After reading this chapter, the participant will be able to:

- Identify risk-management guidelines for nursing documentation
- Explain the consequences of incomplete nursing documentation
- Identify key components to include when documenting an adverse event
- Identify risk-reduction strategies

Your documentation: Truth or consequences?

Some of you may remember a game show entitled *Truth or Consequences*. The clinical record can be very much like that game show. Either "the truth"—in this case, a complete account of the clinical care of the patient—must be present in the medical record, or you and your organization will suffer "the consequences"—an accusation of substandard, fraudulent, or poor-quality patient care.

The truth

The clinical record needs to serve as an accurate and complete accounting of the care rendered. Think of it as a book, or as the story of a patient's care at any point in time: It should have a beginning, middle, and end. Missing chapters leave the reader feeling cheated.

Any reviewer reading a clinical record should get a good clinical picture of the events, care, and outcome relative to the patient. There should be no incomplete flow sheets or graphic sheets and no lapses in progress notes. The record should include the correct date, time, and accounting of the clinical status, as well as the clinical care provided. Do not neglect the simple items—although the date and time of the assessment may seem inconsequential to the nurse, their absence can be used later to demonstrate that a critical element was missing at a critical time in the patient's care.

Consider the following questions:

- How can you prove that your documentation entry was timely?

- How do you prove that your assessment and intervention were based on the patient's condition at that time?

- If those preceding you also did not document the date and time, does that show a pattern of documentation that is unsafe in this day and age of litigation? Does it demonstrate that clinical documentation is not valued?

The truth about the patient's care, the level of competency of the healthcare provider, and the commitment to safe, quality care are all in the clinical record. Therefore, ensure that your clinical records:

- Tell the complete story of care delivered

- Reflect high-quality, nonnegligent care

- Clearly reveal progress or lack of progress towards clinical outcomes

If they are complete, your clinical records will serve as the best defense against allegations of negligence. They are therefore critical legal documents, which means that healthcare professionals have a legal duty to maintain accurate and complete—and sufficiently detailed—clinical records. They should describe acts, events, diagnoses, and conclusions, and they should do so at the time of care because the clinical record is considered trustworthy if the entries are made at the time (provided that they meet established standards or policies).

A jury will assume that the documentation in the clinical record is true. However, this presumption of truth can be challenged if there is any question of quality or alteration of the clincial record (Weinstock and Johnson, 1999).

Nurses often view documentation as a necessary but dreaded task. Home health care nurses need to understand that their detailed documentation can have a very positive impact on the outcome of a case whether for legal, quality, reimbursement, or regulatory reasons.

OASIS coding: Always tell the truth

Since the 1990's home health care agencies have come under scrutiny for fraudulent practices. You may have heard about a practice called "upcoding." This practice is when the OASIS is recorded in a way that would increase payment to a home health care agency. Incorrect and inflated coding is considered a fraudulent action. A nurse's license may be suspended or revoked based on fraudulent practices. Citing that you were told to do it will not hold up as a plausible excuse during an investigation. In today's climate of accountability the nurse can no longer claim ignorance about how to accurately complete the OASIS. Questions regarding how to accurately complete the OASIS can be answered. Each state has a state-based OASIS education coordinator (Madigan, 2006).

The OASIS data is used as a basis for determining your agency's patient case-mix for PPS. With the emphasis on measurable outcomes the OASIS forms the foundation for the CMS' OBQI (Outcomes-Based Quality Improvement) initiative, which should be part of every home care agency's quality improvement program. The OASIS data has legal implications as well. Based on the nurse's admission assessment, the subsequent documentation of care the clinical record must demonstrate that the specified patient needs were met or document the reasons why they were not met. If the clinical record does not support this there may be ramifications, such as:

- Legal liability for substandard care

- Inconsistencies between OASIS assessment and documented patient care may be perceived as fraudulent

- Discrepancies between OASIS data and patient care delivered may contribute to decertification from participating in Medicare and Medicaid

- The individual nurse may be at risk for disciplinary action by state licensure boards (Yadgood, 2005)

One way to ensure that you are keeping up to date with the OASIS changes is to continuously participate in some form of education. One noteworthy Web site is *www.oasistraining.org*. Click on **Reference** in the lower-left corner, then click on **Important Resources.**

Risk management guidelines for documenting care
To create a presumption of good care, there has to be a well-documented clinical record. The following risk-management guidelines may help with this effort:

- Document all care given. This documentation will be measured by the state Nurse Practice Act and standards of professional nursing practice. It is also proof that care was, in fact, given.

- Document conversations with providers and payers. Include highlights of the conversation; the time at which the contact occurred; and the provider's response, instructions, and orders.

- Document the nursing interventions that occurred before and after notifying the provider.

- Never use the clinical record as a battleground.

- If the chain of command was used (notifying your supervisor of clinical services), document who was contacted, the time of the contact, the message communicated, and the response.

- Always complete all forms/documentation tools.

- Document patient instructions given, and conversations held with the patient/family/
  caregiver.

- Use only the accepted methods for correcting charting errors in the medical record.

- Do not document opinions.

- Never blame another individual or department in the clinical record (Greenwald, 2003).

The consequences

Nursing staff often view documentation as a tedious and time-consuming task that adds little value to their daily work. Florence Nightingale wrote, "If a patient is cold, if a patient is feverish, if a patient is faint, if he is sick after taking food, if he has a bedsore, it is generally the fault not of the disease, but of the nursing" (Cahill et al., 1992). Her epidemiological studies demonstrated that nursing has a significant impact on the patient's progress. Consequently, when nurses observe and intervene on behalf of patients, they are responsible for documenting these actions in the medical record (Adamsen and Tewes, 2000).

As a professional nurse or supervisor of clinical services you must recognize that neglecting this documentation could have a profound effect on patient care. Given that the entire healthcare team reviews the clinical record to ascertain the status of and subsequent interventions needed for a patient, missing information may affect the practice of other professionals.

An incomplete and inaccurate medical record also leaves an organization and the nurse vulnerable. It:

- Demonstrates that care was incomplete

- Reflects poor clinical care

- Illustrates noncompliance with the organization's policies

- Supports allegations of negligence

- Supports allegations of fraud

Comprehensive nursing documentation is the most important tool in avoiding allegations of malpractice. It can save you and your staff. When a nurse gives oral testimony about an incident or fact and there is no documentation to support this oral testimony, then the nurse has to try and explain why there is no such documentation if the fact was so important. Any oral testimony without supporting documentation lacks reliability (Ashley, 2004).

Many nursing malpractice cases illustrate the consequences of an incomplete medical record.

Legal risks with IV therapy

"Infusion therapy–related lawsuits are among the fastest-growing category of litigation brought against nurses" (Rosenthal, 2005). Lawsuits can be filed for insertion, infiltration, and phlebitis issues.

Sample legal case:

In February 2001 a man suffered extensive burns to his face, neck, and hands. The EMS staff started an IV in the right arm. However, the IV was not removed or replaced until eight days after admission the man developed a serious infection and had to have surgery. The man cited that the nurses who treated him breached the applicable standard of care, which caused the injury to his right arm (*Health Law Week*, 2007).

The nurse must document all aspects of care with regard to IV therapy. There are established standards, Infusion Nursing Standards of Practice, published by the Infusion Nurses Society and the Centers for Disease Control and Prevention. At least 12 of the 72 current standards apply for home infusion therapy. Be sure your policies, protocols, and documentation form include these standards. When looking at nursing documentation and developing an audit tool, remember that accurate, concise documentation is your best defense.

Look for nursing documentation that includes:

- Type, brand, and length of vascular access device

- Date and time of insertion

- Number and location of attempts

- Site care, including specific site preparation

- Type of IV therapy (drug, dose, rate, time, route)

- Patient's response to therapy

- Barriers to care

- If more than one catheter/lumen is being used, identify each and indicate what fluids/ medications are used for each (Gorski, 2006)

Continuous assessment:

- Patient's tolerance of the IV therapy

- Site appearance (use a standardized scale for this assessment)

- Site care, including dressing changes and equipment per protocol

- Patient/family education

- Discontinuation of the therapy

- Any communication with other healthcare team professionals related to the IV device (Rosenthal, 2005)

Legal risks in skin care

One of the hottest areas of litigation involves wound care. Nurses in home health care are especially vulnerable as the primary provider and evaluator of the condition of the wound. The following factors increase the risk for alleged malpractice:

- Standards for wound care change. The nurse needs to keep up to date with the latest changes.

- Patients/family think the wound develops only because of negligent care and the lack of following appropriate standards of care.

- Use of alternative or "folk medicine" as part of the wound care regimen.

- Failing to follow the physician's/prescriber's orders.

- Carrying out prescriber orders that are an inappropriate treatment plan.

- Failing to monitor and observe a patient properly.

- Not reporting changes in condition to the practitioner.

- Not documenting all care provided.

- Not providing proper care (Hess, 2005).

Here are some strategies to avoid being held liable. You need to protest any decisions of denial of payment and document that protest. Be sure to obtain a valid informed consent, especially for relatively invasive types of wound care. And the most important step: Document all wound care provided (Hess, 2005).

A good documentation system, whether a paper or electronic flow sheet, can assist a nurse in describing the skin, wound characteristics, and other related factors that may be contributing to the progress or lack of progress in healing. The clinical record should include not only the qualitative description of the wound but also any "underlying medical conditions-such as poor nutrition, diabetes, or neuropathy" (Hess, 2005).

There are many good wound care documentation formats on the market. Just be sure that they include the same descriptors found in the OASIS skin and wound status items:

- Anatomic location

- Classification of the wound/staging

- Status of healing; e.g., fully granulating

- Edema

- Exudate amount, color, consistency, and odor

- Odor, if applicable

- Color and temperature of the surrounding skin

- Type of tissue exposed (Hess, 2005)

Case-mix tips

- ICD-9-coding requires that pressure ulcers be coded specific to the location on the patient's body.

- If the bed of the pressure ulcer is covered by necrotic tissue you cannot document the stage of the wound until the necrotic tissue is removed.

- A pressure ulcer becomes a surgical wound if it has a muscle flap.

- Do not reverse-stage a pressure ulcer. Once a pressure ulcer has reached Stage 3 or 4 it can never be recorded at a lower stage. If a 3 progresses to a 4, then it remains a 4.

- Stage 3 and pressure ulcers should be recorded as such for the remainder of the patient's life, even if the ulcer closes or heals.

M0440 Does the patient have a skin lesion or an open wound?

No	Yes
Patient has a healed Stage 1 and no other pressure ulcers or skin lesions/wounds	Patient has some residual scar tissue formation
Patient has a healed Stage 2 and no other pressure ulcers or skin lesions/wounds	
Patient has no scar tissue formation from the healed Stage 2	

Case-mix tips (cont.)

M0445 Does this patient have a pressure ulcer (cont.)

No	Yes
Patient has a healed Stage 1 or 2 and no other pressure ulcers	

(Gaboury, 2006)

Handling documentation errors

If a nurse makes a documentation error, there is an accepted method of correction.

First, check any existing organizational policies or procedures regarding charting errors. If you cannot find anything in writing, call your supervisor/manager. There should be established guidelines for you to follow. These guidelines will ensure consistency and establish common practice for your organization. If you use a computer documentation system, any entries after your initial entry will be captured as "edited." Any changes made in a computerized system note the date and time the entry was altered.

General guidelines for correcting documentation errors include the following:

1. **Write "mistaken entry."**

    In the past, we corrected any charting errors by writing the word "error" near the mistake. The standard today is to write "mistaken entry" above a line drawn through the words that need to be deleted. The entry's date, time, and author's initials should be written above "mistaken entry."

2. **Keep original entry intact.**

    Never scratch out or attempt to obliterate the previous entry. It gives the appearance of someone trying to "cover up" and could cast doubt as to the integrity of the writer and the content of the entire medical record. A single line through the entry with the time, date, and writer's name is appropriate. This way, the original entry can still be read. Sometimes, it is of benefit to write the reason for the correction. For example, "Mistaken entry, wrong medication name written."

3. **Write "late entry" if an entry must be entered late.**

    The writer should document like this: "7/24/07 2:30 p.m. Late entry for 7/24/07 10:00 a.m." Then continue with the documentation that was intended for the earlier time.

4. **Avoid altering numbers or words.**

   Never try to change a word or number into the one you intended. Handwriting experts may be asked to testify that the word or number was changed, and if it was, it can give a false impression of fraud.

5. **Make corrections promptly.**

6. **Review the following example:**

~~7/24/07 1320 Ambulated with assistance to BR. First void post delivery,~~
~~clear yellow urine, no pain with voiding.~~
                                                          ~~P. Jones, RN~~

7/24/07 1325 Mistaken entry above, charted on wrong patient.
                                                          P. Jones, RN

Adverse events: When bad things happen to good nurses

The public expects safe and responsible care whenever entering the healthcare system. They hold everyone in it responsible for the good as well as the poor outcomes of the care they received.

If an organization has a systematic, well-coordinated quality and risk-management program, it demonstrates to the public a commitment to safe and responsible care. In addition, if an organization builds its policies, practices, and guidelines on evidence-based standards, it reduces its risk of liability.

The most cited reference related to patient safety is the Institute of Medicine's (IOMs) November 1999 report, *To Err is Human: Building a Safer Health System*. The report states that between 44,000 and 98,000 people die in hospitals each year due to medical errors—defined as "failure of a planned action to be completed as intended or the use of a wrong plan to achieve an aim"—that were preventable. In response to this report the Institute for Healthcare Improvement (IHI) launched the 100,000 Lives Campaign. The Campaign demonstrated an unprecedented effort on the part of hospitals to reduce preventable patient deaths. The Campaign pushed us to look for better ways to care for our patients and measure our outcomes.

The most common problems that occur during the course of providing patient care include adverse drug events, infections, suicide, falls, burns, and pressure ulcers. Incidents with serious consequences are most likely to occur in the hospital; however, patient care errors can occur in any nursing care setting.

In addition to the legal costs, medical errors cost the nurse in terms of lost confidence, fear, and anxiety of not being able to provide the best care possible. The loss of public trust places the nurse in a vulnerable position, saying that the nurse, not the "system," is to blame.

We have not yet cultivated a blameless approach to medical errors. Until we regain the trust of the public by creating safe, foolproof patient-care systems, medical errors will continue to become claims of malpractice or negligence. Supervisors of clinical services or nurse managers will be held accountable for ensuring safe patient-care processes, and nurses will be held accountable for providing safe patient care.

Therefore, when an adverse event occurs, it is important to follow the organization's policy regarding responding, reporting, and recording. If you are in a nursing management role you will be held accountable for an event if you do not follow the policy as stated. It is everyone's responsibility to be completely knowledgeable of your organization's quality and risk-management policies. Read each of the case scenarios in the following exercise (Figure 2.1) and circle Y if you think the event needs to be reported. Circle N if you think it does not need to be reported.

Figure 2.1 Quiz: Do I need to report this?

1. During ambulation of a patient, the patient hits the bedside table with his arm.	Y	N
2. Your home health aide reports that a patient was found on the floor.	Y	N
3. Shortly after administering a medication to your patient you noted a mild reaction of a rash, itching, and skin warm to touch.	Y	N
4. During a procedure, the equipment involved did not function properly.	Y	N
5. Postpartum neurogenic bladder unresolved at discharge.	Y	N

Answers 1–5: Yes

Whenever there has been an adverse event, the organization's policies will be reviewed by the department of public health, the board of nurse examiners, and the attorneys, if the case raises evidence of negligence. You can protect yourself against culpability by ensuring:

- Accurate documentation in the clinical record

- Accurate incident reporting

- Compliance with established policies

- Assistance in the follow-up investigation

Documentation of adverse events

When an adverse event occurs, emotions are high and critical thinking may be clouded. The nurse must document accurately and completely. Think in terms of where, what, when, why, and how.

Where do you document? Because timeliness and accuracy may become critical in a malpractice case, always have an ample supply of the required documentation forms on hand, in the field and office. These forms may include incident/occurrence forms, progress notes, and investigation forms for the immediate response that was taken as a result of the event.

Keep guidelines and organization policy in the file with the forms. You may even have a template explaining what forms are to be completed, where they are to be sent, and any other essential steps to assist in the completion of the documentation. These steps will help the writer through the adverse-event process in a systematic, orderly fashion.

What do you document? After an adverse event, nursing management is responsible to review the documentation and assist the nurse with suggestions when needed to ensure an accurate and factual accounting. Whatever is documented will need to be reviewed immediately following the event by the quality and risk-management departments, the physician, possibly the patient/family, and others.

What is written at the time of the event may have to stand on its own merit for as long as five years—the case, if pursued by the patient/family, may take that long to go through the legal process. I have always suggested that the nurse read his or her own documentation after it is written. Will it make sense to any reader? Will I remember the intent of the documentation if it is called into question? The documentation must be **f**actual, **o**bjective, **c**omplete, and as **a**ccurate as possible to decrease the liability risk. (Remember the acronym FOCA.) Documenting an accurate date, time, and sequence of events is the best defense to any questions of lapse in care. If your organization's policy does not want the medical record to note the filing of an incident report in the progress notes, ensure that the nurse complies with the policy.

Be sure the nurse's charting creates a reliable timeline. The nurse must carefully note the timing of key changes in the patient's condition. This will assist the nurse in demonstrating that there was a quick response and appropriate measures taken to the crisis.

Tips

Here are some tips to ensure complete charting:

- Note the time the change of condition or crisis began.

- Document the name of the healthcare provider called, the time called, when the provider responded, and when the patient was seen by the provider.

- Chart as soon as possible after care was given.

- Note all provider visits and consultations, whether by telephone or in person. Be sure to include any relevant discussion and new orders as well as nursing actions (Halliday, 2005).

When do you document? Document as soon after the actual events as possible. Many times, the nurse is tired and stressed by the event that occurred and therefore doesn't document it right away. Timeliness is critical in these cases; the nurse must document the event and complete the required documentation elements as close to the time of the event as feasible. Although late entries are an acceptable form of documentation, they may raise questions in the case of adverse events.

Why do you document? Documentation needs to be part of a nurse's delivery of patient care, not apart from it. There is a Chinese proverb that says, "The palest ink is better than the strongest memory." The reason for documentation is clear: Memory often fails us when we put it to the test in a malpractice case. Completing the medical record and any organizational forms that are required as a consequence of an adverse event decreases the likelihood of risk of liability. As stated in Chapter 1, the medical record is considered a legal document. The reason "why" we document is multifaceted. In the case of the adverse event, the "why" is simple: If it was documented, then it was done.

How do you document? As a nurse it is your responsibility to ensure that you use the appropriate form and documents findings in ink. Always ensure the accuracy of the clinical record, and do not alter your progress notes even if you are asked to do so. The nurse must document truthfully and objectively.

> **Tips**
>
> - Verify that the patient's identifier is present on each documentation sheet
> - Record the date and time of each entry
> - State only what was seen and heard (no opinions)
> - Be as specific as possible
> - Use only abbreviations from the organization's accepted list

If you are a nurse manager/supervisor of clinical services and were involved in any way with a potential adverse event or patient/family complaint, you should also document your intervention and outcome. This demonstrates your level of interaction with the staff, patient, family, or physician, and indicates an attempt to work with the staff or patient in the specific event.

Remember that there is never any justification for altering the clinical record after the fact. Clinical record tampering can and will be uncovered by forensic chemists, handwriting experts, or, in the case of computerized medical records, computer experts who are asked to analyze a record whenever tampering is suspected. If record tampering is detected, it will render the clinical record indefensible.

Incident reports

You may think that incident reports are more trouble than they are worth—but think again.

We work in high-stress, fast-paced environments. It is your responsibility as a member of the healthcare team to understand not only the importance of the incident report, but how to critically review an incident to avoid any further occurrences. Your own investigation will also provide possible defense if during your investigation you identified a system failure and took the necessary corrective action(s).

The purpose of the incident report is to refresh the memories of anyone involved. While the clinical record is patient-focused, the incident report is incident-focused. The benefit of the incident report is that years after the event, the incident report will help you and the persons involved remember what happened.

Personal notes and memory joggers

You should never create notes at home concerning the event. You should not discuss the event with other care providers without having someone from risk management present, unless the discussion is in a quality-review process or in the presence of the facility's attorney. "Information given outside of these formats will be considered discoverable by an opposing attorney" (Carroll and Harryman, 1999).

Tips for writing an incident report

In many states, the incident report can be reviewed by the plaintiff's attorney. Therefore, it is important that you and your staff keep in mind that others may read it.

Write objectively:

- Record who and what applies

- Record details in objective terms

- Describe what was seen and heard

- Describe only actions that were performed at the time of the event (e.g., assessment of injuries, assistance back to bed, physician present)

Include essential information:

- Record where, when, and who applies

- Record what the patient said about the incident

- Record the time and place of incident

- Record physician contact

Avoid opinions:

- Do not give your opinion on how it could have been avoided

- Speak to the nurse manager, supervisor, or risk manager

Avoid the blame game:

- Do not use incident reports to blame others

State only what happened:

- Avoid statements like, "Home health aide was late"

File report promptly and properly:

- Send to the designated department per organization policy (Weinstock and Johnson, 1999)

Documenting incidents in the clinical record

When documenting an incident in nursing progress notes, give a factual account of the incident, including treatment and any follow-up care that was provided. Document the patient's response to the care. Doing so shows that the patient was closely monitored after the incident and that the patient received appropriate care.

If the patient or family stated something about their role in the incident, be sure to include it not only in the incident report, but also in the progress notes. For example, if the patient stated, "I know you told me to use the walker, but I thought I could do it alone," the defense attorney may be able to use the quote to prove that the patient contributed to the negligence. In this situation, the patient would be considered guilty of contributory or comparative negligence.

Risk-reduction strategies

- Be sure that everyone is clear as to who is managing the patient. This is especially critical in complicated cases with numerous consults. One of the major factors in adverse events is fragmentation or lack of clear communication between providers. Therefore, use the clinical record as a communication tool for all providers. Be sure and read notes from other providers and disciplines.

- Be sure staff understand and utilize the chain of command when necessary. They are considered patient advocates and must speak on behalf of the patient to ensure quality patient care. Documentation of the chain of command process should be factual and blameless.

- If an adverse event occurs, the staff must know that attention to patient needs is first and foremost. If a patient is injured, nursing and medical interventions take precedence over everything else.

- Follow the organization's policy on medical-event disclosure. It is important that staff understand who is designated to inform the patient/family. Documentation should include who was present during the discussion, what information was discussed, and all of the patient/family responses.

- Ensure that the patient/family receives compassionate care and that everyone involved maintains a professional relationship.

- If an adverse event occurs, contact the risk manager or designated person for your agency. Discuss the case discreetly, because conversations are not protected under a quality statute or attorney-client privilege, and therefore may be discoverable (Rubeor, 2003).

Resources

Accreditation Commission for Health Care, Inc. 2003. *Home Health Accreditation Manual,* 4th ed. Raleigh, NC: Accreditation Commission for Health Care, Inc. *www.achc.org.*

Community Health Accreditation Program, Inc. "CHAP Standards and Self Studies Order Form." *www.chapinc.org/chap-soe.htm*

Department of Health and Human Services. *OASIS User's Manual. http://cms.hhs.gov/OASIS/.asp.*

The Joint Commission. 2007. *Comprehensive accreditation manual for home care.* Oakbrook Terrace, IL: The Joint Commission. *www.jcrinc.com*

References

Adamsen, L. and M. Tewes. 2000. "Discrepancy between patient's perspectives, staff's documentation and reflections on basic nursing care." *Scandinavian Journal of Caring Sciences* 14(2):120–129.

Ashley, R. 2004. "Legal counsel: How do I avoid being sued?" *Critical Care Nurse* 24(6):75–76.

Cahill, J., et al. 1992. *Nurse's Handbook of Law and Ethics.* Springhouse, PA: Springhouse.

Carroll, M., and M. Harryman. 1999. "Documentation and nursing malpractice: What you document today can protect you tomorrow." *Nursing Spectrum* 11A (16):14–15.

Gaboury, M. 2006. *Home Health Pocket Guide to OASIS: A Reference Guide for Field Staff.* Marblehead, MA: HCPro.

Gorski, L. 2006. "Integrating standards into practice." *Home Healthcare Nurse* 24(10):629.

Greenwald, L. 2003. "Malpractice and the perinatal nurse." Journal of Perinatal & Neonatal Nursing. 17(2):101–110.

Halliday, A. 2005. "Creating a reliable time line." *Nursing2005* 35(2):27.

Health Law Week. 2007. "Patient's nurse malpractice vicarious liability claim against hospital may proceed." Strafford Publications, Inc. Accessed 6/14/07 via LexisNexis.

Hess, C. 2005. "The art of skin and wound care documentation." *Home Health Nurse* 23(8):502–513

Madigan, E. 2006. "OASIS Coding, Your License, and Your Reputation" *Home Healthcare Nurse* 24(3):190.

Institute for Healthcare Improvement. 2005. "Overview of the 100,000 Lives Campaign." Available at *www.ihi.org/IHI/Programs/Campaign/100kCampaignOverviewArchive.htm.*

Greenwald, L. 2003. "Malpractice and the perinatal nurse." Journal of Perinatal & Neonatal Nursing. 17(2):101-110.

Rosenthal, K. 2005. "Documenting peripheral IV therapy." *Nursing2005* 35(7):28.

Rubeor, K. 2003. "The role of risk management in maternal-child health." *Journal of Perinatal & Neonatal Nursing* 17(2): 94–111.

Weinstock, D., and P. Johnson. 1999. *Mastering Documentation,* 2nd edition. Springhouse, PA: Springhouse.

Yadgood, M. 2005. "Solving the mystery: The role of competency assessment in OASIS documentation" 23(4): 224–231.

Contemporary nursing practice

Learning objectives

After reading this chapter, the learner will be able to:

- List the components that make up contemporary nursing practice
- Discuss the importance of being familiar with professional nursing standards
- Explain the impact of professional and regulatory standards on contemporary nursing practice
- Identify strategies to employ professional and regulatory standards

Are you using contemporary nursing practice?

Contemporary nursing practice is a combination of the following:

- Nursing knowledge, based on evidence-based standards
- Demonstrated competency
- Demonstrated critical thinking
- The ability to capture these in the medical record

When you practice state-of-the-art nursing, your patient satisfaction scores will reflect a trust and confidence in the organization and satisfaction with the healthcare experience. Measurable clinical nursing outcomes will demonstrate that safe and quality patient care was delivered.

Use the checklist in Figure 3.1 to find out if you are doing all you can to ensure and document contemporary nursing practice in your department or unit.

Figure 3.1	Contemporary nursing practice self-assessment
Do I promote contemporary nursing practice in my department or unit?	❑ As a nurse manager, I ensure that the most up-to-date nursing standards are part of our delivery of patient care ❑ I use professional standards and current nursing research when developing practice guidelines, documentation tools, and policies specific to my patient population
Is contemporary nursing practice reflected in my nursing documentation?	❑ I take into account resources such as the Joint Commission standards, state and federal regulations, and other written professional standards when developing new documentation tools
Do I meet the current standards and expectations for nursing management?	❑ I am certified by the American Nurses Credentialing Center (ANCC) in my specialty (e.g., pediatrics, medical-surgical, perinatal, home health) ❑ I have achieved the highest level of education required for the position ❑ I belong to a professional nursing association ❑ I review my job description annually to ensure that it meets contemporary nursing management standards and review any professional publications specific to nursing management ❑ I attend at least one professional seminar per year ❑ I expect my staff to perform at their highest level when given appropriate direction and resources ❑ I ensure that all new staff have adequate orientation to their position ❑ I recommend extension of the orientation/learning period until I am satisfied that the nurse can provide competent patient care ❑ I fairly evaluate my staff based on concrete evidence of performance ❑ I inform them of areas of concern and assist in their process to meet the mutually agreed-upon goals (when necessary) ❑ I encourage quality improvement as demonstrated in our monitored quality outcomes and in compliance with documentation policies
Does my staff practice state-of-the-art nursing?	❑ I have several nurses who are certified by the ANCC ❑ I encourage the staff to belong to a professional association, achieve the highest level of nursing education, attend continuing-education sessions, be up-to-date on any new or revised policies and procedures, participate on hospital committees, and read current nursing literature ❑ We employ evidence-based nursing practice in our day-to-day patient care ❑ My staff complete hospital-required competency/skills testing ❑ Documentation on the unit is in accordance with the established policies

As professionals, we are held to high standards by the public, regulatory, and legal arenas. There are established professional standards that are used when the care of the patient is in question. Therefore, contemporary nursing practice takes into account our compliance with professional standards, such as the state Nurse Practice Act, the American Nurses Association's (ANA's) *Code of Ethics* and *Nursing Scope and Standards of Practice*, as well as any specialty nursing association's written standards. Evidence of contemporary nursing practice also depends on demonstration of competence based on your level of nursing education, recent continuing education, and certification in a specialty area.

Certification

Certification is one way a nurse can show that he or she either possesses a level of knowledge in a specialty beyond an entry level or has achieved an advanced level of practice. There are three types of certification available to nurses: professional nursing certification board/organization, state certification, and institutional certification. There are more than 30 nursing organizations with certification programs, including the American Nurses Credentialing Center (ANCC), the American Board for Occupational Health Nurses, and the American Academy of Nurse Practitioners.

The most universal type of certification is offered by a professional nursing-certification board. In 1973, the ANA established such certification with the ANA Certification Program. It was implemented to provide a tangible recognition of professional achievement in a defined functional or clinical area of nursing. The ANCC was established as a separate incorporated center and continues to be responsible for administration of the certification process. Its goals include the promotion and enhancement of public health through the certification of nurses. ANCC utilizes the ANA's *Scope and Standards of Nursing Practice* in its credentialing programs.

Certification is based on education, knowledge, skills, competence, and a certification examination for a defined specialty. Once certified by ANCC, for example, a nurse must complete a rigorous reapplication process to remain certified. There are ANCC certification exams for all levels of professional nursing: advanced practice (nurse practitioners, clinical specialists, and other disciplines, such as palliative care), baccalaureate and higher specialties, and diploma/associate-degree specialties.

There is also certification for case managers. The Commission for Case Manager Certifications (CCMC) conducted a study of nurses' roles and functions in the practice of case management. The research described in an article by Tahan, et. al. significantly contributes to the knowledge in the field of case management. "It has described the domains of practice of case managers and the related knowledge required for the work they do. The findings have numerous benefits, including the identification and validation of the roles, functions, activities, and knowledge areas of case management . . . " (Tahan, 2006). Home healthcare nurses can use the identified core components to ensure that they are practicing contemporary nursing. By maintaining the necessary skills and competencies, the home healthcare nurse contributes to patient and agency-based outcomes.

Figure 3.2 features a competency-based performance review.

Figure 3.2 | **Essential case management activities**

	Meets	Does not meet	Needs improvement
General			
Maintains patient privacy and confidentiality			
Adheres to professional ethical standards			
Adheres to legal, regulatory, and accreditation standards			
Serves as an advocate for your patient/family's healthcare needs			
Maintains the patient's safety			
Determines the presence of advance directives			
Assessment			
Reviews information about the patient's condition (e.g., diagnosis, history, prognosis)			
Identifies cases with high-risk potential for complications			
Identifies cases that would benefit from additional types of services such as disease management, PT			
Performs appropriate assessment of the patient or situation using established case management standards			
Interviews the patient to ascertain baseline and ongoing level of physical, emotional, psychological, and spiritual functioning			
Assesses the patient's social support system and relationships			
Assesses for multicultural issues and health behaviors that may affect the patient's health status			
Assesses the need for environmental modifications to address accessibility barriers			
Planning			
Documents and communicates assessment findings to key stakeholders, such as providers, payers, family, etc.			
Establishes treatment goals that meet the patient's healthcare and safety needs			

| Figure 3.2 | Essential case management activities (cont.) |

	Meets	Does not meet	Needs improvement
Establishes, in collaboration with key stakeholders, the goals, objectives, and expected outcomes with time frames			
Reviews requirements for prior approval of services by payer			
Reviews the health history of the patient to ensure accuracy and completeness (you conduct a self-audit)			
Evaluates the ability and availability of the designated caregiver to deliver the needed services			
Utilizes evidence-based practice guidelines in development of the plan of care			
Determines how to handle cultural factors that might affect the plan of care			
Reviews all documentation for completeness and accuracy			

Implementation

Implements the plan of care efficiently			
Communicates the plan of care to key stakeholders			
Analyzes the plan of care for cost-effectiveness			
Engages patient/family to actively participate in the development of goals			

Coordination

Utilizes evidence-based practice guidelines in the development of the plan of care			
Establishes working relationships with referral sources			
Documents the implementation of the plan of care			
Educates the patient/family about wellness and illness prevention strategies specific to the condition			

Monitoring

Consults with other members of the home health care team			
Monitors the patient's progress in achieving the goals/outcomes in the plan of care			
Documents the patient's progress in achieving the goals/outcomes in the plan of care			
Monitors utilization management activities, such as authorization for services			
Monitors disease management activities			
Appeals service denials			

Figure 3.2	Essential case management activities (cont.)

	Meets	Does not meet	Needs improvement
Evaluation			
Evaluates the effectiveness of the plan of care based on identified goals			
Evaluates and documents the patient's use of/response to therapeutic interventions			
Documents the patient/family response to interventions			
Evaluates the timeliness and availability of treatments and services (this measures variances)			
Evaluates the impact of multicultural issues as related to health behaviors and the plan of care			
Analyzes outcome data such as clinical, financial, quality, and patient satisfaction			
Outcomes			
Examines the effectiveness of case management on the plan of care and patient outcomes			
Evaluates actual patient outcomes in relation to expected outcomes			

Adapted from Tahan: et al. "Case manager's roles and functions: Commission for case manager certification's 2004 research, Part I." *Lippincott's Case Management* 11(1):16–19.

Professional standards

Nurses must recognize that regardless of whether they choose to become a member of a professional nursing organization, the established and recognized standards written by the organizations are used as the official legal standard.

The ANA standards are used to describe general and specialty nursing practice competency. All professional nurses should become familiar with these standards in addition to their organization's standards of nursing practice. Every profession has established guidelines, standards, and recommendations that are used when questions are raised about the professional and his or her action in question. The profession of nursing is no exception.

Standards of practice:

- Are authoritative statements developed by professional nursing associations

- Detail the responsibilities, values, and priorities of the nurse

- Hold nurses legally and ethically accountable

- Are vital to all practicing nurses

- Provide guidance in clinical settings

- Provide expectations for competence

- Are used in professional negligence cases

- Are used by state boards of nursing to evaluate allegations of violations of the state's Nurse Practice Act

The ANA's *Scope and Standards of Nursing Practice* was first published in 1973. The standards focused on the nursing process as a critical-thinking model for all registered nurses. The 2004 *Nursing: Scope and Standards of Practice* includes the following:

- Scope of nursing practice

- Standards of nursing practice

- Standards of professional performance

The scope and *Standards of Nursing Practice* clearly articulates what is expected of every practicing nurse.

The standards directly correlate to the nursing process. The documentation of each step is critical in proving that something was, in fact, done to the patient. If the expected care is not documented, the plaintiff's attorney will suggest that it was not done at all, and there is no supporting documentation to prove otherwise.

Case study

Misconduct

A new nurse to the home healthcare field was terminated after she administered a medication she was unfamiliar with to a patient. She did not know what the medication was intended for nor the possible side effects. The nurse did not use a reference source for finding the necessary information. She was fired for misconduct (*Legal Eagle Eye Newsletter,* 2007).

Case study

Termination for lapses in IV technique

A home health agency in Maine terminated a home care nurse because of two lapses in IV technique. "As required by law, the agency also sent the state board of nursing a detailed statement of its reasons for terminating this nurse" (*Legal Eagle Eye Newsletter*, 1997).

Quality clinicians are using evidence-based practice supported by research and expertise to guide their clinical decision-making. As a home healthcare nurse, you have already used one of the most common clinical guidelines—care and treatment of the patient with a pressure ulcer. This guideline was developed by the Agency for Healthcare Research and Quality (AHRQ).

The lack of adherence to any evidence-based clinical guideline would not only yield poor patient outcomes, but also speak to the competency level of the practicing nurse. The nurse would not be demonstrating contemporary nursing practice and standards of care.

The ANA also has published standards for nurse managers in the *Standards of Practice for Nurse Administrators*. If you are a nurse manager, you should be familiar with the established expectations of the "registered nurse whose primary responsibility is the management of healthcare delivery services and who represents nursing services" (ANA, 2004). Your major responsibility is the "implementation of the vision, mission, philosophy, core values, evidence-based practice, and standards of the organization, and nursing services within their defined areas of responsibility" (ANA, 2004).

Your performance as a manager is based on whether you perform the following in relation to quality nursing documentation:

- Participate in nursing and organizational policy formulation

- Accept organizational accountability for services provided

- Evaluate quality and appropriateness of nursing care

- Ensure appropriate orientation, education, credentialing, and continuing professional development for staff

- Provide guidance for and supervision of personnel accountable to the nurse manager

- Evaluate performance of staff

- Ensure shared accountability for professional practice (ANA, 2004)

Code of ethics

In addition to the professional standards of nursing, a nurse should be aware of another bench-mark for the profession of nursing. The ANA's *Code of Ethics for Nurses with Interpretive Statements* was revised in 2001. It is mentioned in this chapter about contemporary nursing practice because it is the ethical standard by which a nurse is judged.

The *Code of Ethics* is for all nurses, and it:

- Reiterates the fundamental values and commitments of the nurse

- Identifies the boundaries of duty and loyalty

- Describes the duties of the nurse that extend beyond individual patient encounters

"Whatever the version of the Code, it has always been fundamentally concerned with the principles of doing no harm, of benefiting others, of loyalty, and of truthfulness" (ANA, 2001).

Provision 3 of the *Code* holds the nurse accountable for ensuring patient rights and safe care: *"The Nurse promotes, advocates for, and strives to protect the health, safety, and rights of the patient"* (ANA, 2001).

The provision also includes interpretive statements. For example, interpretive statement 3.4, entitled "Standards and Review Mechanisms," holds all nurses to ensuring that only individuals who demonstrate competency, commitment, and integrity are allowed to enter into and continue to practice within the profession. It goes on to state:

"The nurse has a responsibility to implement and maintain standards of professional nursing practice. The nurses should participate in planning, establishing, implementing, and evaluating review mechanisms designed to safeguard patients . . ." (ANA, 2001).

Provision 4 holds the nurse accountable for his or her practice and the obligation to provide optimum patient care, even when there is a delegation of tasks. The interpretive statements of Provision 4 clearly identify what the nurse is being held accountable for:

- Acceptance of accountability and responsibility

- Accountability for nursing judgment and action

- Responsibility for nursing judgment and action

- Delegation of nursing activities

Provision 5 holds the nurse responsible

"to preserve integrity and safety, to maintain competence, and to continue personal and professional growth" (ANA, 2001).

As you can see, contemporary nursing includes many components that the nurse must meet in order to state that he or she practices contemporary nursing.

State Nurse Practice Act

Whether you are a nurse manager or a practicing home healthcare nurse, you are evaluated as to whether you demonstrate contemporary nursing practice. Your first duty is to ensure that you know and understand your state Nurse Practice Act.

The state Nurse Practice Act will define what is expected of nurses when they provide nursing care. It may define what each level of nurse is for that state. It may also define the responsibilities and functions of the nurse. For instance, the state Nurse Practice Act will often delineate the registered nurses' (RNs') accountability and level of responsibility in that state. Nurses need to understand what their level of accountability is, especially when working with unlicensed assistive personnel. If RNs do not understand or comply with the state Nurse Practice Act, they leave themselves vulnerable to action against their professional licenses.

Copies of your state's Nurse Practice Act are usually available at the State Board of Nursing or State Department of Public Health Web site. You can find your State Board of Nursing through the National Council of State Boards of Nursing (*www.ncsbn.org*).

Similar to national professional standards, the state Nurse Practice Act will also define nursing practice based on the following nursing process, which was discussed in Chapter 1:

- Assess health status and record health data
- Analyze and interpret said recorded data
- Make informed decisions
- Plan and implement nursing intervention/evaluate outcomes of nursing intervention and initiate change

Example

Massachusetts State Nurse Practice Act

Definition of *registered nurse:*

"Registered Nurse is the designation given to an individual who is licensed to practice professional nursing, holds ultimate responsibility for direct and indirect care, is a graduate of an approved school for professional nursing, and is currently licensed as a Registered Nurse pursuant to M.G.L.c. 112."

It goes on to dictate registered nurses' responsibility:

"Included in such responsibility is providing nursing care, health maintenance, teaching, counseling, planning, and restoration for optimal functioning and comfort of those they serve."

Under the heading "Responsibilities and Functions":

"A registered nurse shall bear full and ultimate responsibility for the quality of nursing care she/he provides to individual and groups."

And in relation to delegation of nursing activities:

"... May delegate nursing activities to other registered nurses and/or health personnel, provided that the delegating registered nurse shall bear full and ultimate responsibility for

> *making an appropriate assignment;*
>
> *properly and adequately teaching, directing and supervising the delegate; and*
>
> *the outcomes of that delegation."*

As this example shows, the RN in Massachusetts is held accountable for patient care regardless of whether he or she chooses to delegate the nursing activity. Therefore, competency level and contemporary nursing practice is incumbent on both the nurse assigned and the person to whom the activity is delegated. The grounds for disciplinary action against a nurse's license are broad in scope, but the most common are:

- Incompetence or negligence in performing a nursing duty
- Falsification of medical records or insurance claim forms
- Physical or verbal abuse of the client
- Substance abuse
- Illegal conduct

(Monson, 2001)

Threats to licensure

A single complaint against a nurse can trigger an investigation of a nurse's practice. The complaint can be filed by a patient, colleague, physician, or hospital administrator. The board of nursing is the agency responsible for regulating the practice of nursing in each state and has a duty to investigate all allegations.

As a conscientious nurse, it is your responsibility to ensure that you know the scope of nursing practice and the set expectations for a RN. There could be allegations that you breached your

state Nurse Practice Act, that you did not meet the "just and prudent" nurse measure, or that your practice violated state, federal, or professional standards. All of these will be analyzed to evaluate your nursing action in question. In many cases, your only defense will be what nursing actions were taken, which should be in the nursing documentation. Studies have demonstrated time and time again that nurses do not value the time and effort needed in documentation, but as you can see, it is a critical element that you may need in a time of licensure review or alleged malpractice.

Whenever a case and the medical record are reviewed by external reviewers (e.g., state department of public health surveyors, the board of nursing or the board of medicine, or by a patient's attorney), there is potential for action against your nursing license. If the investigator agrees with the complainant that the nurse poses a clear and immediate danger to the public's health and safety, there will be disciplinary action. Disciplinary action could include:

- Censure
- Letter of reprimand
- Probation (time defined)
- Suspension of license
- Revocation of license

Pertinent clinical records, human resource files, and copies of the organization's policies and procedures will all be reviewed. The board of nursing may also ask an independent nurse consultant to review the nursing documentation and determine whether the nursing actions were appropriate.

> ### Example
>
> ### Examples of disciplinary categories:
>
> - Substandard nursing practice not involving medications (e.g., verbal abuse, failing to respond to changes in patient condition)
> - Destruction or alteration of patient records (e.g., fraudulent charting, signatures, or replacement of records with intent to mislead or deceive)
> - Physical patient abuse
> - Failure to follow policy
> - Controlled substance violations/chemical dependency
> - Impaired mental or physical competency
> - Sexual misconduct
> - Patient/employer abandonment
>
> (Clevette, 2007)

Professional boundaries in home care

According to Wright, "Professional boundaries allow for a safe and therapeutic relationship between the nurse and the patient." Of course, this is an acceptable definition. However, in home healthcare, the risks of crossing this professional boundary are high. Home healthcare nurses must always maintain a professional relationship with the patient/family and not move into a personal relationship. Because home healthcare nurses work in autonomous settings and in the privacy of a patient's home, they must be diligent in keeping the relationship on a professional level.

Again, according to Wright, "the role of a State Board of Nursing is to protect the public from unsafe nursing care, and nurses who fail to establish and maintain professional boundaries in home care can be reported to the board of nursing for alleged violations of the state nurse practice act and board of nursing regulations" (2006).

Here are examples of boundary violations that involved home care nurses in Ohio:

- During a skilled visit for two-year-old twins, a home care nurse lost control and yelled and spanked the children

- A home care nurse had her name on the patient's bank account

- A home care nurse engaged in a sexual relationship with a patient

- A home care nurse obtained the patient's property and assets

- A home care nurse discussed personal problems with a patient and received many items, such as money, furniture, a TV, a cell phone, and clothing, from the patient

- A home care nurse became sexually involved with the father of a pediatric patient (Wright, 2006)

Federal and state regulations

It is the responsibility of everyone in nursing to know and develop processes and systems to comply with licensing and accrediting standards established by federal or state regulatory bodies. Compliance with these standards decreases the likelihood of lawsuits, as it demonstrates that the care provided to the patient was consistent with recognized standards.

State regulations are critical for continuing licensure. Each state has established regulations that mandate guidelines for patient care, staffing requirements, qualifications for key positions, and documentation elements necessary to demonstrate compliance. It is your responsibility to keep up to date with the regulations and any documentation elements required. Techniques for integrating state, federal, and Joint Commission standards will be discussed in later chapters.

If a deficiency is cited when a surveyor evaluates an agency in relation to the state regulations, the agency is required to write a plan of correction. In a case where malpractice is alleged, any noncompliance with the state regulation could be cited as the cause of injury. Therefore, it is essential for the nurse to ensure that the agency's policies, protocols, and documentation tools are constantly in compliance. Continuous quality improvement strategies (e.g., ongoing audits of identified weak documentation elements) can assist you in this area.

Likewise, federal regulatory laws are also exact and prescriptive. The Centers for Medicare & Medicaid Services (CMS) sets patient care guidelines for all areas.

Hospitals: Sec. 482.23 Condition of Participation: Nursing services

(3) A registered nurse must supervise and evaluate the nursing care for each patient.

(4) The hospital must ensure that the nursing staff develops, and keeps current, a nursing care plan for each patient.

(5) A registered nurse must assign the nursing care of each patient to other nursing personnel in accordance with the patient's needs and the specialized qualifications and competence of the nursing staff available.

(6) Nonemployee licensed nurses who are working in the hospital must adhere to the policies and procedures of the hospital. The director of nursing service must provide for the adequate supervision and evaluation of the clinical activities of nonemployee nursing personnel that occur within the responsibility of the nursing service.

Source: *Conditions of Participation*, 2004

Just as at hospitals, nurses at long-term care facilities and home healthcare agencies are expected to render care in accordance with the regulations of both federal and state governments. These standards are contained in the *Code of Federal Regulations* (42 CFR, Parts 430 to end). The Omnibus Budget Reconciliation Act of 1987 (OBRA), a national law specific to long-term care facilities, was developed to establish consistent standards for all facilities across the country. The standards require that facilities must demonstrate Medicare and Medicaid compliance in order to receive funding.

The conditions of participation for long-term care facilities and home health agencies are as follows:

Long-term care facilities: Sec. 483.30: Nursing services

The facility must have sufficient nursing staff to provide nursing and related services to attain or maintain the highest practicable physical, mental, and psychosocial well-being of each resident, as determined by resident assessments and individual plans of care.

Source: *Code of Federal Regulations*

> ## Example
>
> ### Home health agencies: Sec. 484.30 Condition of participation: Skilled nursing services
>
> The [home healthcare agency] furnishes skilled nursing services by or under the supervision of a registered nurse and in accordance with the plan of care.
>
> (a) Standard: Duties of the registered nurse. The registered nurse makes the initial evaluation visit, regularly reevaluates the patient's nursing needs, initiates the plan of care and necessary revisions, furnishes those services requiring substantial and specialized nursing skill, initiates appropriate preventive and rehabilitative nursing procedures, prepares clinical and progress notes, coordinates services, informs the physician and other personnel of changes in the patient's condition and needs, counsels the patient and family in meeting nursing and related needs, participates in inservice programs, and supervises and teaches other nursing personnel.
>
> Source: *Code of Federal Regulations*

Regardless of the setting, nurse managers are responsible for ensuring compliance with the state and federal regulations that rely heavily on documentation in all areas of the medical record, such as admission assessments and development and adherence to the plan of care.

The Joint Commission

According to The Joint Commission, its mission is to "continuously improve the safety and quality of care provided to the public through the provision of healthcare accreditation and related services that support performance improvement in healthcare organizations."

Joint Commission accreditation can be beneficial by:

- Leading to improved patient care

- Demonstrating the organization's commitment to safety and quality

- Substituting for certification surveys for Medicare and Medicaid

- Fulfilling licensure requirements in many states

The Joint Commission has standards and performance measurements that gauge the organization's level of performance in the areas of patient rights, patient treatment, infection control, performance improvement, and others.

Because Joint Commission accreditation is recognized nationwide as a symbol of quality, the use of its standards in revising and building a good documentation system can be of great benefit. Although The Joint Commission will not prescribe what type of documentation tool to use, it will read the clinical record to validate that you meet Joint Commission standards.

CHAP accreditation

Your agency may be Community Health Accreditation Program (CHAP)–accredited. CHAP surveyors also perform Medicare compliance activities. They determine whether an agency meets the Medicare *Conditions of Participation* (CoP) in addition to the CHAP accreditation requirements. "The CHAP Standards of Excellence, driven by consideration of management, quality, client outcomes, adequate resources, and long-term viability, are the basis for accreditation" (Fineout, 2004).

As a staff nurse in an agency preparing for a CHAP survey, use the following checklist.

Example

Preparing for CHAP certification: Staff nurse checklist

❏ Learn as much as you can about CHAP.

❏ Learn your agency's accreditation goals.

❏ Know your agency's assessment, admission, transfer, and discharge policies and procedures. Be sure to document accordingly.

❏ Learn about the Medicare requirements (*CoPs*) if your agency is Medicare-certified.

❏ Follow the patient's plan of care.

❏ Document your supervisory visits when there is a home health aide assigned and stay within the standards.

❏ Follow bag- and hand-washing policies.

❏ Prepare the patient/family for a surveyor site visit through appropriate education, reinforcement of teaching, and documentation of such.

(Fineout, 2004)

Organizational policies and procedures

Your organization's policies and procedures constitute some of the most important sources for standards of care. Staff will be held accountable for knowing the policies and any revisions.

Your agency should have all policies on file—any policy that was in place at the time of an incident, even from previous years, must be preserved. The policy and expected standard of care defined in that policy will be used in any legal case. The nurse manager or administrator will be asked to speak about it during a deposition and during litigation.

Tips for leading your staff in contemporary nursing practice

As our industry rapidly changes, so too must our patient-care policies, standards, and practices. Our nursing practice must reflect evidence-based care, contemporary nursing standards, and knowledge of the regulatory and accreditation bodies. If you are a member of the nursing management team, you are responsible for mentoring your staff and ensuring that they deliver contemporary nursing practice. Do the following:

- Post a copy of the state Nurse Practice Act in the staff lounge.

- Ensure that you stay current on nursing practice by tracking nursing trends through nursing journals and the Internet. Assign two staff members per month to report on one new nursing trend during staff meetings.

- Purchase copies of the professional standards for your nursing specialty. Buy one copy for the agency and one copy for your office. Use it when revising job descriptions or policies.

- Join a professional nursing organization(s). Understand that despite the often high cost and frequent lack of organizational reimbursement, the benefits outweigh the costs in the long run.

- Be aware of new/revised policies. Encourage your agency to have a "read and sign" system for the agency's records. If certain staff members do not read or sign posted policies, this should be reflected in an annual performance review. A track record of reading and becoming informed about new and revised policies will help you in any legal case.

Remember that sources of standards of care can include:

- State Nurse Practice Act

- Professional nursing organizations

- State Board of Nursing

- State regulatory statutes

- Accreditation organizations (e.g., The Joint Commission)

- Organizational policies and procedures

- Requirements of third-party payers

- Court decisions

Competency assessment

It was once thought that once a nurse graduated from nursing school and was practicing, he or she was "competent." This idea was challenged in the early 1990s by The Joint Commission, which began to require that all nursing staff demonstrate competency regardless of their title or years in nursing practice. The Joint Commission wanted to ensure that competent healthcare providers were caring for the public. Now other regulatory and accreditation bodies require competency assessments for nonclinical and clinical providers.

Miller defined competency assessment as a "process that assesses the level of knowledge, skills, and motivation needed for an employee to adequately perform the duties of [his or her] assigned role to a given standard" as delineated by the employee's performance standards (2006).

A good example of the above definition would be the competency of the home care nurse who also completes the OASIS. The home healthcare agency screens all new staff members and provides orientation to the OASIS process. The agency must also provide periodic retraining. Because the OASIS meets the competency selection guidelines of being high risk, high volume, problem prone, and high cost, the staff needs to be competent in many nursing skills. An inaccurate OASIS assessment can result in fiscal and quality implications as well as a reflection on you as a nurse and your professional commitment to patient care (Yadgood, 2005).

As a competent home healthcare nurse can you say that you have the following core practice competencies.

Core competency	Yes	No
Assessment skills		
Intervention skills		
Effective communication skills		
Critical-thinking skills		
Human care and relationship skills		
Management skills		
Leadership skills		
Patient/family teaching skills		
Knowledge integration skills		

(Yadgood, 2005)

Disease management in home healthcare

Another way to demonstrate that you practice contemporary nursing care is by using evidence-based practices. Disease management has been promoted in the acute care settings for years. The home healthcare setting is ripe for employing or referencing theses guidelines in nursing care. There are common elements to the definition of disease management: "These definitions view *disease management as an approach to delivering healthcare to persons with chronic illnesses that aims to improve patient outcomes while containing healthcare costs*" (Huffman, 2005). So, as you can see, disease management fits perfectly into home healthcare. In fact, disease management focuses on the populations that home healthcare nurses see in the community, such as patients who have:

- Congestive heart failure (CHF)

- Diabetes

- Chronic obstructive pulmonary disease

- Falls

- Osteoarthritis

- Depression

- Medication management (Peterson, 2004)

These target diseases have current clinical practice guidelines that are accessible to all healthcare providers. In fact, Peterson identifies six practices from the clinical practice guidelines that can yield immediate results for home healthcare agencies:

1. Standardized clinical pathways for decreasing rehospitalization in CHF patients

2. Multifactorial risk assessments for all patients

3. Exercise programs for patients with knee osteoarthritis

4. Standardized depression screening tools

5. Pharmacist involvement in medical management

6. Telemedicine to promote self-management (Ahrens, 2005)

CMS is also investigating how disease management programs can help with improved patient outcomes as part of its Pay for Performance initiative. With everyone looking at outcomes-driven data as a measure of quality, home healthcare nurses must understand and use evidence-based practice and outcome-based care models. Because diabetes is the sixth leading cause of death and the cost of caring for it is high, your agency may want to focus on this disease first. There are clinical practice guidelines available from the National Guideline Clearinghouse at *www.guideline.gov* and on the American Diabetes Association Web site at *www.diabetes.org*.

> ### Sample
>
> ## Diabetes mellitus evidence-based standards of care
>
> - A1C biannually when blood glucose is controlled
> - A1C quarterly when blood glucose is uncontrolled
>
> Patient glycemic control:
>
> - Self-monitoring of blood glucose
> - Medication management
>
> Implications for the home healthcare nurse:
>
> - Assess availability of blood glucose monitor in the home
> - Patient/caregiver's knowledge of blood glucose monitoring technique and monitoring schedule
> - Patient access to medications (financial, pharmacy access, etc.)
> - Knowledge and ability to take medications as prescribed (Miller, 2006)

Resources

Accreditation Commission for Health Care: *www.achc.org*

ANA: *www.nursingworld.org*

Centers for Disease Control and Prevention (CDC): *www.cdc.gov*

Centers for Medicare & Medicaid Services: *www.cms.hhs.gov*

CHAP: *www.chapinc.org*

Department of Health and Human Services: *www.hhs.gov*

Institute for Healthcare Improvement: *www.ihi.org*

Institute for Safe Medication Practices: *www.ismp.org*

The Joint Commission: *www.jointcommission.org*

National Council of State Boards of Nursing: *www.ncsbn.org*

National Council of State Boards of Nursing: A nurse's guide to the importance of professional boundaries (2004), *www.ncsbn.org/pdfs/ProfessionalBoundariesbrochure.pdf*

National League for Nursing: *www.nln.org*

National Quality Measures Clearinghouse: *www.qualitymeasures.ahrq.gov*

Nurses Service Organization: *www.nso.com*

References

Ahrens, J. 2005. "The need for evidence-based guidelines in home care." *Home Healthcare Nurse* 23(3):147–149.

American Nurses Association. 2001. *Code of Ethics for Nurses with Interpretive Statements.* Washington, DC: American Nurses Publishing.

American Nurses Association. 2004. *Scope and Standards for Nurse Administrators,* 2nd edition. Washington, DC: American Nurses Publishing.

American Nurses Association. 2004. *Nursing: Scope and Standards of Practice.* Washington, DC: American Nurses Publishing.

Centers for Medicare & Medicaid Services. 2001. *Code of Federal Regulations.* Title 42, Public Health, Chapter IV, Conditions of Participation for Hospitals, Part 482, p. 496. Available from *www.cms.hhs.gov.*

Centers for Medicare & Medicaid Services. 2001. *Code of Federal Regulations.* Title 42, Public Health, Chapter IV, Requirements for States and Long-Term Care Facilities, Part 483, pp. 388–389. Available from *www.cms.hhs.gov.*

Centers for Medicare & Medicaid Services. 2001. *Code of Federal Regulations.* Title 42, Public Health, Chapter IV, Conditions of Participation, Home Health Services, Part 484, pp. 441–442. Available from *www.cms.hhs.gov.*

Clevette, A. 2007 et al. "Nursing licensure: An examination of the relationship between criminal convictions and disciplinary actions." *Journal of Nursing Law* 11(1):5–11.

Fineout, C. 2004. "Preparing for CHAP accreditation." *Home Healthcare Nurse* 22(3):156–159.

Huffman, M. 2005. "Disease management: A new and exciting opportunity in home healthcare." *Home Healthcare Nurse* 23(5):290–296.

"Home health: Defamation suit filed by nurse, thrown out by court." 1997 *Legal Eagle Eye Newsletter for the Nursing Profession.*

"Misconduct: Nurse Gave Unfamiliar Med Without Looking It Up, Termination for Cause Upheld." 2007. *Legal Eagle Eye Newsletter for the Nursing Profession,* 15(5):8.

Miller, C. 2006. "Using standards of care to drive evidence-based clinical practice and outcomes for diabetes mellitus." *Home Healthcare Nurse* 24(5):307–311.

Monson, M. 2001. "License to practice: For keeps?" *Nursing Management.* 32(11):21.

Peterson, L. E. 2004. "Strengthening condition-specific evidence-based home healthcare practice." *Journal for Healthcare Quality* 26(3):10–18.

Tahan, H. 2006. "Case manager's roles and functions: Commission for case manager certification's 2004 research, Part I." *Lippincott's Case Management* 11(1):4–22.

Wright, L. 2006. "Professional boundaries in home care." *Home Healthcare Nurse* 24(10):672–675.

Yadgood, M. 2005. "Solving the mystery: The role of competency assessment in OASIS documentation." *Home Healthcare Nurse* 23(4):224–231.

Clinical documentation

Learning objectives

After reading this chapter, the learner will be able to:

- Explain the three major functions of the medical record
- Discuss how documentation helps ensure compliance with regulatory and accreditation requirements
- Discuss where to find the necessary nursing documentation to increase compliance with quality measures

The effects of staff documentation on compliance, quality, and reimbursement

Over the past few years there has been a surge to increase the quality of patient care by looking at outcomes. It is no different in home healthcare. As a case manager, you are now looking at documenting accurate clinical assessments, controlling infection, and providing safe, quality nursing care to demonstrate outcomes for performance improvement reports. The focus is not only on nursing functions but now includes nursing outcomes. Consequently, your documentation is one of the most important aspects used to evaluate nursing performance, reimbursement, and quality patient care centered on evidence-based outcomes.

Nursing documentation serves many purposes. The importance of your documentation cannot be understated, as it is used for:

- Ensuring continuity and quality of patient care through communication
- Furnishing legal evidence of the process and outcomes of patient care
- Supporting the evaluation of the quality, efficiency, and effectiveness of the care given
- Providing evidence for research, financial, ethical, and performance improvement purposes
- Assisting in the establishment of current levels of standards of clinical practice

- Ensuring appropriate reimbursement

- Providing data for other purposes, such as risk-management monitoring (Cheevakasemsook et al., 2006)

Clinical record as communication

You may not believe that your documentation affects everyone who cares for the patient, but you would be mistaken. Every discipline uses various sections of the clinical record—including the nursing documentation—to learn about the patient.

Nurses need to understand that their documentation is as important as that of any other member of the healthcare team. In fact, because the nurse may be the only professional provider who continuously cares for the patient, nursing documentation is the most important part of the clinical record.

Regardless of the setting of care, the patient's nursing care is ultimately the nurse's responsibility. In all patient-care settings, nurses must document in the clinical record for others to read what was seen, heard, and done during that visit.

Besides the clinical-care team, the following individuals, institutions, and agencies also may be involved in reading the clinical record:

- Patients, families, and legal guardians

- Alliances and systems of care

- Peer-review organizations

- Accountants

- Quality-assurance and risk-management companies

- Administrators

- Health maintenance organizations

- Private insurance companies

- Quality-improvement staff

- Government agencies

- Medical-records staff

- Hospice personnel

- Review agencies

- Risk managers

- Acute or long-term care facilities

- Disease registries

- Physician offices

- Attorneys, expert witnesses, judges, and jury members

Every aspect of the patient's care must be documented in the clinical record, in a graphic sheet, flow sheet, progress note, or plan of care. All nursing documentation must be complete and accurate. A well-documented nursing progress note/flow sheet will communicate what the nurse assessed and responded to and what other measures were necessary to care for the patient at that time. It paints a picture of the patient for the reader.

If you are committed to safe and efficient nursing care you should routinely review your own documentation to determine how well you have communicated the patient's care in the clinical record. Ensure that anyone reading the clinical record would be able to understand what occurred during the visit, the adherence to the plan of care, and how the patient is progressing to the specified outcomes.

Clinical record as a demonstration of compliance

External reviewers use the clinical record to evaluate various kinds of compliance.

There are stringent regulations with which the home healthcare clinical record must comply for the facility to remain licensed to receive Medicare/Medicaid reimbursement. Everyone is held accountable for complying with the facility's policy for documentation so that it meets the Centers for Medicare & Medicaid Services' (CMS') standards and *Conditions of Participation* (CoP). Everyone in the organization needs to understand the various functions of the clinical record and its importance to regulatory standards, requirements, and how compliance is evaluated (Zuber, 2004).

Compliance is monitored in various ways. For example, the medical record is viewed by surveyors who review specific focus areas to determine whether the patient received the care required by the state or federal regulations. If a medical record does not contain the necessary documentation, the agency is at risk not only for a deficiency, but also a loss of reimbursement. Loss of reimbursement affects everyone in the organization.

In a Medicare-certified home health agency, the clinical record documentation will be evaluated for compliance with:

- Medicare CoPs

- Compliance with Medicare coverage rules and payment process

- Quality patient care standards (Zuber, 2004)

Compliance with the Medicare CoPs is critical to the financial survival of your agency. Your accurate and timely documentation should demonstrate patient assessments completed within the required time frames, as well as include signed documents denoting the patient was informed of his or her rights and all required notices and advance directives. The patient plan of care (POC, 485) should identify the patient's needs, establish eligibility for Medicare coverage, and describe the treatments and services planned. The POC is a signed physician order and must be returned to the agency within the designated time frame for your state. As for your clinical notes, they need to show that the services recorded in the 485 were provided and within professional standards. Timely documentation of all physician notification of the patient's change in condition or revision of the POC must be evident. In addition to these required documentation elements, you must document care coordination between and within disciplines. As Zuber notes, "other components detailed in the CoPs include signed verbal orders, signed and dated progress notes, summary reports with documentation that the reports were sent to the physician, and a discharge summary with documentation that a copy was offered to the physician (2004)."

Figure 4.1 is a summary of how important documentation supports the functions and requirements of the clinical record.

Figure 4.1	Functions and documentation requirements of the clinical record

Comprehensive assessment	CoPs Compliance
Plan of Care	
Patient rights	
Professional standards, compliance with	
Coordination of care	
Physician orders, compliance with	
Service delivery (nursing, therapy, medical social work, home health aide)	
Clinical record contents	
For Medicare-certified agencies:	Medicare coverage requirements
Medicare coverage	
Homebound status	
Skilled care, need for	
Under the care of a physician	
Receiving covered services	
OASIS data	
Quarterly clinical record review	PI–Performance Improvement activities
Outcome-based quality improvement	

Adapted from Zuber, R. 2004."Back to Basics The Clinical Record", *Home Healthcare Nurse* 22(5):329.

PRO and managed-care standards

Like compliance with CMS standards, compliance with peer-review organization (PRO) and managed-care standards must be reflected in the clinical record. Key elements of the clinical record will be reviewed in an ongoing evaluation of quality patient care, and if the reviewer cannot find evidence of compliance with these standards, you may face denial of payment, or worse, the agency will have to repay. Your documentation will need to demonstrate compliance with the prescribed POC, delivery of services and supplies, adherence to professional standards, and practice of evidence-based care. The managed-care case manager may only authorize a few skilled visits and will need frequent updates on the patient's progress toward agreed-upon goals and clinical progress notes. Here is where your documentation is essential to negotiating more skilled visits. Once you have negotiated for more visits, the clinical record will need to demonstrate that the visits are necessary to keep the patient out of the emergency department or hospital. An example would be a nonresolving congestive heart failure. Critical elements need to be in the nursing documentation. (Refer to "Tips on Documentation, Quality, and Reimbursement" in the Appendix.)

The Joint Commission and 'tracer methodology'

The Joint Commission standards address all aspects of patient care. Joint Commission surveyors review the clinical record for demonstration of quality patient care and compliance with established standards.

In addition to its 2004 standards, The Joint Commission has implemented a new accreditation process: Shared Visions–New Pathways®. The new survey process shifts the focus from survey preparation and score achievement to continuous systematic and operations improvement.

The shift allows The Joint Commission to focus to a greater extent on the provision of safe, high-quality care, treatment, and services. The Joint Commission not only evaluates the quality being provided at a particular facility or agency but posts the results on its Quality Check Web site for public access. These Quality Reports feature a user-friendly format, allowing the public to compare health organization performance in a number of key areas. The Quality Reports provide information about your organization's compliance with the National Patient Safety Goals and performance on the National Quality Improvement Goals (hospitals only). Examples of the National Quality Improvement Goals are heart attack, heart failure, community-acquired pneumonia, pregnancy and related conditions, and surgical infection prevention. Evaluation of compliance with both of these is through medical record reviews (The Joint Commission, 2007).

For the on-site visits, surveyors will analyze your agency's compliance with selected standards and its systems of providing care, treatment, and services. The "tracer methodology" includes the clinical record as a critical component. The surveyor selects a patient, resident, or client, and uses that individual's clinical record as a "road map." He or she traces the care documented to determine whether the agency has complied with standards and systems for providing quality care and services. "Tracing the patient through [his or her] care experience, the home care or hospice surveyor will further focus on standards that are applicable to the priority focus areas (PFAs) that are preselected by The Joint Commission's central office." The surveyor then traces the patient's care from the beginning through to his or her current status—known as *individual patient tracers* (Friedman, 2004). So as you can see, your clinical documentation must demonstrate quality patient care and compliance with CMS and Joint Commission standards.

When selecting individual tracers, surveyors look for patients who are in top clinical/service groups (CSGs) and PFAs for your agency. "CSGs" are "groups of patients in distinct, clinical populations for which data is collected" (CAMHC, 2007).

The CSGs are as follows:

- Home healthcare agencies:
  - Home health services
  - Home personal care/support services
- Hospice providers:
  - Facility-based respite care
  - Facility-based symptom relief
  - Hospice in-home care
- Medicare-certified home health agencies:
  - Patients having:
    - ~ Acute care hospitalizations
    - ~ Confusion difficulties
    - ~ Emergent care
    - ~ Pain interfering with activity
    - ~ Stabilized bathing
  - Patients needing:
    - ~ Ambulation improvement
    - ~ Bathing assistance
    - ~ Oral medication management
    - ~ Toileting assistance
    - ~ Transferring assistance
    - ~ Upper-body dressing assistance

First the clinical record will be reviewed at the point at which the patient currently is receiving care. Then it will be reviewed from the point of admission to any point in which the individual received care, treatment, or services. In addition to examining the clinical record, the surveyors will speak with any of the providers who provided the care to that tracer patient. If during the course of this review a surveyor identifies a compliance issue or a pattern of noncompliance with a specific issue, the surveyor may review additional clinical records. The additional review will attempt to identify whether the issue is isolated or whether it represents a larger system issue for the organization.

The Joint Commission National Patient Safety Goals and the National Quality Improvement Goals are also part of the survey process. Figure 4.2 outlines the 2007 Joint Commission Home Care National Safety Goals.

Figure 4.2	The 2007 Joint Commission Home Care national patient safety goals	
Goal	**Description**	**Essential Documentation**
1	**Improve the accuracy of patient identification.** Use at least 2 patient identifiers when providing care, treatment, or services.	The patient was identified when administering medications or collecting lab specimens for clinical testing.
2	**Improve the effectiveness of communication among caregivers.**	
2A	For VO or TO or for telephone reporting of critical test results, verify the complete order or test result by having the person receiving information record and "read-back" the complete order or test result.	"Read back" per agency policy. Suggestion: date, time and person results were given.
2B	Standardize a list of abbreviations, acronyms, symbols, and dose designations that are not to be used throughout the organization.	Compliance demonstrated through chart audits. Staff follow the agency's "do not use" list.
2C	Measure, assess, and, if appropriate, take action to improve the timeliness of reporting, and the timeliness of receipt by the responsible licensed caregiver, or critical test results and values.	Critical tests and reporting are noted in clinical record to be delivered within the agency's policy.
2E	Implement a standardized approach to "hand off" communications, including an opportunity to ask and respond to questions.	Documentation or evidence that the "hand off" communication included up-to-date info re: patient's care, treatment and services, condition and any recent or anticipated changes.
8	**Accurately and completely reconcile medications across the continuum of care.**	Medication list initiated at admission with patient/caregiver involvement. Medications list is always up-to-date and a copy in the home.
9	**Reduce the risk of patient harm resulting from falls.**	Fall risk patients identified at admission and during service. Initiation of fall reduction strategies in the clinical record.
13	Encourage patients' active involvement in their own care as a patient safety strategy.	Conversations, education regarding safety (equipment, fire) or other concerns of safety.
15	The organization identifies safety risks inherent in its patient population.	Safety/risk assessment completed at admission and as needed during service.
15B	The organization identifies risks associated with long-term oxygen therapy such as home fires.	Conversations, education regarding safety (equipment, fire) or concerns of care, treatment, services. Level of comprehension and compliance Communication of concerns with MD Home safety risk assessment Oxygen safety factors

Quality and risk-management review

Quality and patient safety have taken a front seat in all areas of nursing. The Institute for Healthcare Improvement (IHI) has pushed this agenda and helped us stay focused on quality patient outcomes. The IHI is a not-for-profit organization leading the improvement of healthcare throughout the world. In a recent report, *Status quon't: Why health care will never be the same*, it cites organizations that have tackled patient care issues and systems successfully (IHI, 2007). Quality clinical care is tightly associated with quality documentation.

The departments of quality and risk management and your agency's quality improvement team will review the clinical record for compliance with the organization's policies, procedures, protocols, standards of practice, quality indicators, and peer-review requirements. They may also review the clinical record as part of a complaint investigation and adverse medical event. In such cases, the documentation in the clinical record will assist these departments' reviewers in determining whether the care provided was appropriate, complete, and timely. If the facts in the clinical record are clear, the case will be easy to defend.

Figure 4.3 outlines compliance chart reviews.

Figure 4.3 Compliance chart review table	Investigation of an adverse event	Complaint investigation	Quality review
Established organization policies, procedures, protocols, guidelines	X	X	X
Standards of nursing care	X	X	X
Evidence-based standards	X	X	X
Mandated standards: Joint Commission, state, federal, insurers	X	X	X

Documentation in the clinical record needs to reflect all of the above, because it will come under scrutiny during an investigation or in the process of monitoring compliance with quality measures. As stated in previous chapters, the proof is in the clinical record. The presence and quality of documentation will substantiate compliance with established practices; its absence or lack of quality will leave the nurse vulnerable, having to defend his or her assertions that good nursing judgment and practice was used.

In home healthcare, the National Quality Forum (NQF) uses 15 standardized performance measures. The Centers for Medicare & Medicaid Services will report data from these measures in its public report card, Home Health Compare (*www.medicare.gov*/HH*Compare*). These standards may also be used by home healthcare providers for their internal quality improvement efforts as well as by researchers and regulators. The NQF measures are:

- Improvement in ambulation/locomotion

- Improvement in bathing

- Improvement in transferring

- Improvement in management of oral medications

- Improvement in pain interfering with activity

- Improvement in status of surgical wounds

- Improvement in dyspnea

- Improvement in urinary incontinence

- Decrease in number of pressure ulcers

- Emergent care for wound infections, deteriorating wound status

- Emergent care for improper medication administration/side effects

- Emergent care for hypo/hyperglycemia

- Acute care hospitalization

- Emergent care

- Discharge to community (NQF, 2005)

As you can see, nursing documentation is crucial to measuring the patient's progress toward or avoidance of some of these quality indicators.

Figure 4.4 features an example of how this information is acquired.

Figure 4.4		NQF information gathering		
Measure	**Source**	**Numerator**	**Denominator**	**Exclusions**
Improvement in status of surgical wounds	OASIS/OBQI 2,3,4	Patients for whom: • The value of OASIS item M0488 at discharge from home healthcare is lower numerically than the value of the same item at the start or resumption of care **OR** • The value of OASIS item M0482 or M0440 at discharge from home healthcare is 0, and the value of M0482 at the start of or resumption of care is 1	Patients for whom: • The value of OASIS item M0482 at the start of or resumption of care is > 0 **AND** • The value of OASIS item M0488 is not equal to "NA–No Observable Surgical Wound"	• Nonresponsive at start or resumption of care • Episodes of home healthcare ending with admission to an inpatient facility or death • Maternity patients • < 18 years of age

Source: *NQF National Voluntary Consensus Standards for Home Health Care.* Appendix A: Specifications of the National Voluntary Consensus Standards for Home Health Care, A-4.

There are currently 41 home health quality indicators. Of these, 30 are deemed *risk-adjusted* and 11 are *descriptive* quality measures. The risk-adjusted outcome measures are those used to compensate for differences in the patient population served by different home health agencies. The descriptive outcome measures are not risk adjusted and observe all eligible patients served by home health agencies. The data is aggregated to obtain a national observed rate (accessed 6/2/07, *www.cms.hhs.gov/HomeHealthQualityInits/10_HHQIQualityMeasures.asp#TopOfPage*).

Clinical record as a path to reimbursement

As well as being used as evidence of compliance with standards, the clinical record is also used to obtain reimbursement for the care rendered. This reimbursement could come from private, managed-care, or federal- and state-approved payers.

The medical-review analysts for the Medicaid PRO spend hours reviewing medical records, for example, of Medicare and Medicaid recipients. They review these records specifically to ensure that government-paid services are medically necessary, that care was provided in the appropriate setting, and that care was within the accepted medical standards. The overall goal of the review, however, is to ensure that the Medicaid patient received good care.

A reviewer will note any positive or negative findings in the reviewed medical record (e.g., missed set of vital signs). Most citations come from charting deficiencies. For example, if the clinical record contains poorly written progress notes, incomplete flow sheets, lack of uniform abbreviations, and illegible handwriting, the reviewer has no choice but to cite the facility. If the pattern continues and the citations become numerous, the organization could lose federal funding (Raymond, 2002).

Similarly, in home healthcare, documentation links closely to federal compliance and reimbursement. Documentation is used to validate the need for continued home healthcare services and continued reimbursement. Poor documentation can lead to a loss of revenue due to denied claims by the insurer, or can force staff to spend additional time correcting illegible or incorrect documentation. The following components of documentation are essential for agency reimbursement:

- Sound database with a complete medical history

- An acceptable diagnosis(es)

- An appropriate plan of treatment

- A complete care plan

- Accurate progress notes reflecting achievement of the stated outcomes on the plan of care

- Correspondence of history, diagnosis, and problems listed on care plan with physician orders

- Completion within the prescribed schedule

In the future, home healthcare will also be paid for effective performance. The pay for performance will be linked to actual activities and efforts of the home health providers using evidence-based practices and systems. Hence, complete and accurate documentation will be necessary to demonstrate compliance, quality, and eligibility for appropriate reimbursement.

Reimbursement, quality, and documentation are all linked. The insurer is looking for compliance with safe, competent, quality care. If the documentation in the clinical record demonstrates that the care rendered meets quality standards, then reimbursement for the services will be delivered.

Tips

Tips for coding OASIS

1. Be sure coding, OASIS, and 485 all align for optimal reimbursement.

2. Use the OASIS/Medicare language to show the patient's condition. This will prevent monetary penalties.

3. Complete timely documentation for all visits, as this ensures timely reimbursement.

4. Be sure your insurance authorizations are correct to avoid billing errors and promote timely payment for services.

5. All MO items with an asterisk (*) point toward the PPS score and should always be documented in written clinical findings.

MO390 Vision*	Answers 1 and 2 add points to PPS score	Needs to be verified in written clinical findings
MO420 Frequency of pain affecting activity/ movement*	Answers 2 and 3 add points to PPS score Pain must affect activity or movement to be scored here	
MO450 and MO460 Multiple pressure ulcers, most problematic*	Add PPS points with two or more Stage III or IV Add PPS points with any pressure sore	
MO476 and MO488 Stasis ulcer status, surgical wound status*	Add PPS points with partially granulated or nonhealing	
MO490 Shortness of breath*	Always have the patient demonstrate; do not accept his or her word for it If the patient uses continuously or over 50%, make this assessment with O2 If only wears intermittently, check without O2	
MO520 Urinary incontinence*	If checked in MO220, mark it here as well unless corrected by surgery or healed urinary tract infection Any amount of incontinence counts	
MO540 Bowel incontinence*	Boxes 2 to 5 add points to PPS score	
MO550 Ostomy for bowel elimination*	Boxes 1 and 2 add PPS points	
MO610 Behaviors demonstrated at least once a week*	If you checked memory affecting safety or impaired decision-making in MO220, check this item as well	

Tips

Tips for coding OASIS (cont.)

MO650 and 660 Ability to dress upper and lower body*	Answers 1, 2 or 3 add points to PPS Answer should reflect the patients' ability to obtain and put on their clothing	Needs to be verified in written clinical findings
MO670 Bathing*	Answers 2–5 add points to PPS	
MO680 Toileting*	Answers 2–4 add points to PPS score	
MO690 Transfers*	Answer 1 adds less than boxes 2–5 to PPS score	
MO700 Ambulation/ Locomotion*	Boxes 1 and 2 add fewer points than boxes 3–5 to the PPS score	

Source: Adapted with permission from *Bristol Hospital Home Care.*

Clinical record and pay for performance

For years, the home health industry has used the OASIS data for reimbursement. Now the OASIS data and supplemental nursing documentation is being used for payment based on the quality of care provided. The pay-for-performance program will be rewarding for those home healthcare agencies that are efficient and sustain or improve their patients' outcomes. The OASIS data is the basis for pay for performance, so it is essential that the staff ensure accurate data. In addition to an initial orientation, the agency will need to provide annual competency evaluations to ensure that the OASIS data is consistent and precise. To supplement staff members' education, there is a free Web training available at *www.oasistraining.org*. The value of peer review, chart reviews, and interrater reliability should not be underestimated. Review of specific OASIS questions should be posted or discussed during the monthly staff meetings. In addition to staff competency, the agency should also be looking at employing clinical pathways that have achievable, measurable outcomes. Evidence-based, standardized care processes are a sure method of ensuring quality. A good clinical pathway will have patient education as a large component, as the goal is self-care management (Niewenhous, 2007).

Resources

Centers for Medicare & Medicaid Services: *www.cms.hhs.gov*
Reporting hospital quality data for annual payment update and hospital quality initiative information

The Medicare Quality Improvement Community: *www.medqic.org*
Quality improvement organization directory and quality improvement resources and strategies

www.medicare.gov/HH Compare/Home.asp
Consumer information on home healthcare quality initiatives.

www.qualitycheck.org
Comprehensive guide to the nearly 15,000 Joint Commission–accredited healthcare organizations and programs throughout the United States

References

Cheevakasemsook, A., et al. 2006. "The study of nursing documentation complexities." *International Journal of Nursing Practice* 12(6):366–374.

Friedman, M. 2004. "Tracer methodology and the new Joint Commission Home Care and hospice survey process." *Home Healthcare Nurse* 22(10):710–714.

Institute for Healthcare Improvement (IHI). 2007. *Status quon't: Why health care will never be the same.* Available at *www.ihi.org/NR/rdonlyres/858C562A-A535-4344-9573-3AACD1E01CA1/0/2007ProgressReportFINAL.pdf.*

"National Voluntary Consensus Standards for Home Health Care: A Consensus Report." Available at *http:216.122.138.39/pdf/reports/home_health.pdf*

Niewenhous, S. 2007. "How does 'quality' fit in 'pay for performance'?" *Home Health Care Management and Practice* 19(2):91–93.

The Joint Commission. 2007. "Facts About Quality Check and Quality Reports." Available at *www.jointcommission.org/ qualitycheck/06_qc_facts.htm.*

Raymond, L. 2002. "Documenting for the PROs." *Nursing2002* 32(3):50–53.

Zuber, R. 2004. "Back to the basics: The clinical record." *Home Healthcare Nurse* 22(5):327–332.

Nursing negligence: Understanding your risks and culpability

Learning objectives

After reading this chapter, the learner will be able to:

- Define the legal terms nurse case managers must understand when considering nursing documentation
- List the major categories of negligence in nursing malpractice cases
- Discuss the legal risks for nurse case managers when an adverse event occurs
- Describe possible high-risk errors in home healthcare

Legal issues

According to Eileen M. Croke, EdD, ANP, LNC-C, more and more nurses are being named defendants in malpractice lawsuits. Citing the National Practitioner Data Bank (NPDB), she claims, "A charge of negligence against a nurse can arise from almost any action or failure to act that results in patient injury—most often, an unintentional failure to adhere to a standard of clinical practice—and may lead to malpractice lawsuit" (Croke, 2003).

Nancy Brent, author of *Nurses and the Law: A Guide to Principles and Applications*, further explains, "Negligence has emerged as the dominant cause of action for accidental injury in this nation" (2001). It has increased medical-malpractice premiums, involved nurses to a greater extent in allegations of malpractice, and raised interest in tort-law reform.

These facts indicate that all nurses must become familiar with the legal aspects of nursing practice and the importance of nursing documentation. Therefore this chapter will review legal definitions and ways in which nurses in home healthcare could be held liable for negligence.

Essential definitions

tort law: The violation of some duty clearly set by law, not by a specific agreement between two parties, as in breach of contract. It includes negligence and professional negligence. A *tort* is a civil wrong for which the law allows the injured party to seek damages.

negligence: Conduct that falls below the standard established by law for the protection of others against unreasonable risk of harm. It includes the concept of foreseeability (i.e., that the harm that occurred could have been anticipated). Measured by "the ordinary, reasonable, and prudent nurse" standard, The Joint Commission defines *negligence* as "failure to use such care as a reasonably prudent and careful person would under similar circumstances" (Joint Commission, 2007).

Professional negligence as defined by Austin is "failure to provide the prevailing standard of care to a patient, which results in injury, damage, or loss to the patient" (2006).

When alleging professional negligence the patient (plaintiff) has the burden of proof. The patient (plaintiff) must prove all of the following elements:

duty: The nurse had a duty to provide care and follow a professional standard of care.

1. **breach of duty:** The nurse failed to adhere to the professional standard of care.

2. **proximate cause:** The nurse's failure to adhere to the professional standard of care caused the injury.

3. **damages or injuries:** The patient did suffer an injury as a result of the nurse's negligent actions (Showers, 2000).

negligence by commission: When an individual does something that an ordinary, reasonable, and prudent person would not do.

negligence by omission: When one fails to do something a duty exists to do.

professional malpractice: Involves an action by a professional that falls below the professional standard of care. The Joint Commission defines it as the "improper or unethical conduct or unreasonable lack of skill by a holder of a professional or official position" (Joint Commission, 2007).

res ipsa loquitur: A rule of evidence that allows for an inference of negligence based on the circumstances surrounding the injury (e.g., foreign objects left in a patient's body after surgery).

liability: Responsibility for the actual loss, evil, or burden for which justice requires the individual to compensate the victim.

vicarious/imputed liability: Responsibility one is found to have for the actions of other individuals because a special relationship exists between those individuals (e.g., employer/employee relationship).

respondent superior: Latin for "let the master answer." The employer is held liable for the negligent acts of employees if the act occurred during the employment relationship and was part of the employee's responsibilities (e.g., the nurse providing care causes an injury, so the injured patient can sue the nurse as well as the employer) (Brent, 2001).

Factors that contribute to malpractice cases against nurses

The healthcare industry is constantly changing to meet fiscal and consumer demands. The acute-care length of stay continues to shorten, the home healthcare patient population is more acute and complex, and the level of accountability expected by the public has heightened. There are several factors that have contributed to the increase in malpractice cases against nurses, according to Croke, including:

- Early discharge of patients from hospitals

- Advances in technology

- Increased autonomy and accountability of nurses

- Informed consumers

- Expanded legal definitions of liability

In her analysis of 350 case summaries, Croke identified six major categories of negligence that lead to malpractice lawsuits. They center on documentation that describes the negligent behavior in terms of "failure to, lack of, incomplete, ineffective, and improper" (Croke, 2003).

Six major categories of negligence that result in malpractice lawsuits

The following six categories of negligence often result in malpractice cases involving nurses:

- **Failure to follow standards of care**, including failure to:
  - Perform a complete admission assessment or design a plan of care
  - Adhere to established protocols or organizational policies and procedures
  - Follow a physician's order

- **Failure to use equipment in a responsible manner**, including failure to:
  - Use the equipment as designated or follow manufacturer recommendations
  - Check the equipment for safety prior to use
  - Place the equipment properly during the treatment
  - Learn how the equipment functions

- **Failure to communicate**, including failure to:
  - Notify the physician in a timely manner when the patient's condition warranted it
  - Listen to a patient's complaint and act accordingly
  - Communicate effectively with a patient/family
  - Seek higher medical authorization for a treatment

- **Failure to document**, including failure to note in the patient's clinical record:
  - The patient's progress and response to treatment
  - Any patient injury
  - Pertinent nursing-assessment information
  - A physician's medical order(s)
  - Information from telephone conversations with physician (including time, content of the conversation between nurse and physician, and any action taken)

- **Failure to assess and monitor**, including failure to:
  - Complete an assessment
  - Implement a plan of care
  - Observe the patient's progress
  - Interpret signs and symptoms accurately

- **Failure to act as a patient advocate**, including failure to:
  - Question any incomplete or illegible medical order
  - Provide a safe environment (Croke, 2003)

Example

Failure to follow MD orders

An elderly home care patient was on Relafen (side effects: GI bleeding). Her home healthcare nurses were having difficulty with managing pressure ulcers. The lab results revealed low hematocrit and albumin levels and a high platelet count. The nurses were less aggressive in their attempts to improve skin integrity and began end-of-life interventions. The physician had ordered urinary catheterization. The nurses did not follow through on the physician's order, as the son allegedly cited that a catheter was not necessary as he was going to ensure that his mother would be kept dry. The nurses were faulted for not following the physician's orders and that it was a significant factor in the continued ulceration of her sacral area due to the continued presence of urine (*Legal Eagle Eye Newsletter*, 2007).

Home healthcare litigation

Most malpractice cases are in the acute and long-term care settings. However, the number of malpractice claims in home healthcare are increasing. This is in part due to the benchmarking of quality outcomes, the increased use of evidence-based guidelines in practice, consumer awareness of standards, and prevention of errors and complications. The patients for whom you care in the community are clinically complex with complex nursing care needs. "In addition, the law now recognizes that nurses are responsible for and make healthcare judgments, and it holds nurses liable for decisions that depart from accepted standards in the community" (Dailey, 2005).

Dailey and Newfield cited the common legal pitfalls for home care nurses are:

- Unsafe admissions

- Incomplete assessments

- Lack of clarifying MD orders

- Lack of attendance at continuing education programs, reading nursing/medical journals, and participating in professional organizations

- Failure to look up unfamiliar medications or doses

- Failure to follow standards of practice (Dailey and Newfield, 2005)

The public has been exposed to the term *adverse event* in the hallmark Institute of Medicine (IOM) report *To Err is Human*. This report increased national interest in the whys and hows of substandard patient care. In home healthcare, the OASIS data contributes to adverse event outcome reports. As CMS cites, "adverse events serve as markers for potential problems in care because of their negative nature and relatively low frequency" (CMS, 2001). Patient care is being monitored through your nursing assessment in the agency's outcome-based quality improvement activities. However, the adverse events are judged as serious negative outcomes and are treated differently from the outcome-based measures in OASIS. This does not preclude the nurse from accurate and timely documentation. The following are examples of adverse event outcomes that require thorough, concise, and timely documentation. They are:

- Emergent care for injury caused by fall or accident at home

- Emergent care for wound infections, deteriorating wound status

- Emergent care for improper medication administration

- Emergent care for hypo/hyperglycemia

- Development of urinary tract infection; increase in pressure ulcers

In home healthcare, the burden of proof that quality care was provided is on the nurse. The home healthcare nurse's documentation needs to demonstrate that the care provided was within the standard of care and that the outcome could not have been prevented. Litigation frequently comes from the home healthcare nurse's failure to communicate significant clinical changes. And because physicians rely more heavily on the nurse's judgment than in any other healthcare setting, the focus in a legal case would be on the nurse.

Newfield cited that "falls and wounds are widely regarded as the major causes of home care litigation." However, he did cite that legal cases from falls in the home are more common, but the wound care cases disfiguring injuries that are distressing to the jurors. One such case was awarded $1.5 million back in 1988 (Newfield, 2005). The home healthcare nurse needs to be especially vigilant in the care and documentation of patients with wounds, falls, IV therapy, and psychiatric imbalance.

Wound care negligence

The role of nurses and the expected use of professional judgment have changed over the years. Nurses are expected to provide safe quality patient care in all healthcare settings. In the cases of wound care negligence, the claims of improper wound care usually come from the alleged failure to follow the physician's orders and from the nurse's lack of sound, "reasonable" nursing judgment. The plan of care must be clear and reflect the patient's condition and the nurse's expectations regarding wound care. Any changes in the plan of care must have corresponding signed physician orders.

Another area of nursing malpractice stems from a nurse's failure to assess the signs and symptoms of infection, change in condition, or nonhealing. Again, documentation is critical to demonstrate competency and adequacy of a nurse's wound care assessment. Newfield gave an example of how even a simple failure to document a patient's temperature could lead to accusation of missing one of the clinical signs of infection. Coupled with the need for accurate documentation is the timely communication of change in patient condition. The home healthcare nurse is exposed to liability until the physician is notified and informed of the wound's condition (Newfield, 2005).

Minimizing exposure to liability is clearly evident in the clinical record. Home healthcare nurses must demonstrate in their documentation that despite clinically sound nursing practice and use of evidence-based guidelines, there are cases in which the patient's wound deteriorates or an infection occurs.

Practical tips

Critical risk-management tools

1. Ensure that the clinical record shows that there was effective communication with all involved—patient, physician, team members, and supervisor.

2. Document the level of involvement of the patient/caregiver and the goals and realistic expected outcomes, including complications.

3. Check for accuracy and timeliness of nursing assessments and progress notes. Be sure to include clinical findings, use of the plan of care, and progress toward established goals. This is especially important for those agencies with electronic clinical records. Use of prompts is acceptable to ensure a thorough assessment, but nurses then fall into a false sense of security by not writing a narrative progress note for significant variances.

Case study

In one case, a Georgia court concluded that the nursing documentation supported that the nursing care was not negligent, as alleged by the patient's family. The nursing documentation in the acute care and skilled nursing facilities prior to discharge to home was carefully examined. The area in question (sacrum) was so well noted that the expert witnesses could not say that the pressure sore was any worse when the patient left the skilled nursing facility. This case points out the legal importance of accurate and thorough nursing documentation (*Legal Eagle Eye Newsletter,* 1997).

Averting legal issues about falls

Falls in the elderly population often result in some type of injury. In fact, one-third of our elderly aged 65 and older fall at least once a year. These falls account for two-thirds of accidental deaths, as well as for nonfatal fractures, lacerations, and head trauma injuries (Smith, 2007). And we know that there are many factors that increase the potential for falls in this population. A fall can result in complications and disabilities. Unfortunately, when a fall occurs in the home in the presence of a home care provider, the presumption is that it should have been avoided. Therefore, you can now understand that the statement that "fall-related injuries are a disproportionate percentage of home healthcare liability claims" (Newfield, 2006).

An aggressive fall prevention program, thorough assessments, accurate documentation, and a performance improvement plan can help an agency argue its commitment to safe patient care.

According to Newfield, an agency must first dismiss the misperception that there was negligence if the fall occurred in the presence of a provider. To address this misperception, he has suggested the following:

- Set reasonable expectations for falls

- Do fall prevention at the start of care and reassess during the course of care

- Identify criteria for allowing independence or limiting risks to falls

- Assess each patient as an individual

- Include the patient's attitude toward assistance, assistive devices, and ambulation

- Discuss with patient/family the risk of falls and the consequences of a fall; the risk can be reduced but not eliminated

- Discuss the need for participation for the fall prevention program to work (Newfield, 2006)

All of the above should also be documented in the clinical record. Establishing a "paper trail" of the expectations of the patient and agency, comprehension, and participation may be crucial at a later time.

Averting legal issues with IV therapy

According to Rosenthal, "infusion–therapy–related lawsuits are among the fastest growing category of litigation brought against nurses" (Rosenthal, 2005). IV therapy is considered "invasive" in nature, and the outcomes resulting from IV therapy problems can be injurious and debilitating. The best way to avoid a possible claim of malpractice is impeccable documentation. Gorski stated that the malpractice cases against home care agencies stem from complications with patient or caregiver administration. In these cases patient education, and documentation of such, is critical (Gorski, 2006). In addition to your documentation skills, you need to ensure that you demonstrate competency and follow the standards published by the Infusion Nurses Society and the Centers for Disease Control and Prevention.

The latest revised *Infusion Nursing Standards of Practice* (SoP) was published in 2006. Twelve of the 72 standards are applicable to home infusion therapy, but the following four are especially related to documentation:

- Standard 1: Practice Setting—the standards should be available in your agency and used in the development of agency policies and procedures.

- Standard 4: Infusion Nurse—defines the educational qualifications of the registered nurse and clinical competency. Be sure you can demonstrate competency in application of technology and its application in the clinical setting, fluid and electrolyte balance, pharmacology, infection control, neonates and pediatrics (if you serve these specialties), transfusion therapy, antineoplastic and biologic therapy, parenteral nutrition, and performance improvement.

- Standard 11: Patient Education—must include documentation of self-care practices, verbal and written instructions given, validation of the learners' understanding, and the ability to perform infusion-related self-care procedures safely.

- Standard 14: Documentation—your documentation skills will protect you and your colleagues if a question of negligence arises. Your documentation should include at least:
  - The type, brand, and length of the vascular access device
  - Date and time of insertion—be sure to include number and location of attempted insertions
  - Site care and site preparation
  - The type of infusion therapy, drug, dose, rate, time, and route
  - Patient's response to the procedure/therapy—include any symptoms and lab tests
  - Any barriers to care
  - For multiple catheters/lumens indicate the fluids/medications given in each pathway

Case study

Behavioral health case study

Working with patients in the community who have behavioral health problems can lead to legal problems. Here is a case from California in which a psychiatric patient attacked and attempted to kill his father. The father filed a civil lawsuit against a corporation that was providing psychiatric care and support to mentally ill adults in the community. The court found that there had been a lack of supervision in the patient's medication compliance. In fact, the patient had made numerous statements threatening to kill his father. The patient's condition was worsening, and he fell into a delusional psychotic state. "When a psychiatric patient reveals intent to harm a specified individual, the patient's caregivers must try to warn the individual, must alert law enforcement, and must start the process to have the patient confined or to keep the patient confined as a threat to others. This legal duty is not limited to licensed psychotherapists or to caregivers who conduct therapy sessions with patients." This opinion clearly holds caregivers, whether licensed or unlicensed, to the legal obligation to warn the victim and take appropriate action. As you can see, documentation of all nursing actions and communication is critical in averting legal repercussion (*Legal Eagle Eye Newsletter,* 2005).

Legal risks for clinical managers

The risks for anyone in nursing management are similar. Although the staff you supervise are held accountable to their own nursing practice, your scope of responsibilities includes monitoring their compliance with organization policies, ensuring safe staffing levels, and enforcing contemporary nursing practice.

There are several potential sources of liability for malpractice against you as the nurse manager. These causes of actions include:

- Negligent hiring

- Negligent retention of incompetent or impaired employees

- Failure to supervise and train staff

- Inappropriate assigning of staff (Connor, 2006)

Therefore, you will be held accountable for providing staff members with appropriate management, supervision, resources, and support to carry out their duties. If an adverse event occurs and the case becomes an allegation of malpractice, the agency risk manager, your agency attorney, and the attorney(s) for the plaintiff may call you in during preparation and ask you to demonstrate your level of competence as the nursing-management representative; your reputation for having sound management style; and a consistent, proactive approach to ensuring safe patient care.

If a case of malpractice does occur, all aspects surrounding the case will be examined:

- Could this event have been prevented?

- Were patient-safety practices enforced?

- What was the competency level of the staff nurses involved?

- Did the staff have adequate supplies and knowledge to prevent the event?

- How was the case managed once the event was discovered?

- Did everyone meet the standards of care when rendering services?

- What led up to the event?

- What was your role in the event, both expected and completed?

Negligent supervision

As a director or clinical manager, you must ensure that patients have appropriate care and that the staff providing the care has appropriate supervision. Therefore, if a patient is injured and suspects that staff was not adequately supervised, he or she will allege that your supervision was negligent.

Your liability for negligent supervision will be based upon any of the following:

- Your assignment of a patient case to a nurse who was unable to perform the care

- Your failure to personally supervise the nurse when you knew or should have known that supervision was necessary

- Your failure to take the necessary steps to avoid patient injury when you should have intervened

When negligent supervision is alleged, you will be held to the "ordinary, reasonable, and prudent" standard. That is, you will be measured against what other clinical managers would have done in a similar situation (Brent, 2001).

Imputed liability

You also could be held accountable for a nurse's actions by the definition of imputed liability. Imputed (or vicarious) liability states that you may be liable because you hired a nurse to provide nursing services on behalf of you and the organization. When your nurse is found guilty of providing negligent care, the agency will likely be held responsible for the burden of compensation, as it is in a better financial position than the nurse. However, it is your responsibility to ensure the hiring of competent staff, as well as their comprehensive orientation, and thorough supervision of all your staff, to reduce the organization's liability.

Manage your risk

In addition to what was done after the event, there will be questions raised as to nursing management's responsibility with regard to maintaining staff competency, adequate work environment, etc. Your job description will be reviewed, in addition to the current standards of practice for anyone in nursing management. Your level of education, certification, and continuing competence will also be questioned.

You must be able to defend your management competency by demonstrating your enforcement of all of the organization's education and training requirements, as well as ongoing enforcement of policies related to patient care. This would be self-evident in the rate of compliance with the completion of job orientation, annual competency and education requirements, and attendance or effective communication with all staff regarding agency and organization business and new policies/practices.

Use the following checklist (Figure 5.1) to help manage your risk when an adverse event occurs.

Figure 5.1 Nurse manager risk-management checklist for adverse events		
Potential questions	Yes	No
1. Did my staff follow organization policies, procedures, and practices?		
2. Was the policy followed in this event?		
2a. If NO, I implemented changes as soon as possible after the event occurred to prevent any other adverse event.		
3. The nursing documentation was reviewed for accuracy and completeness.		
4. The necessary departments were notified of the event (e.g., risk management).		
5. An intensive investigation or root-cause analysis with the staff involved was completed as close to the date of the event as possible.		
6. The necessary changes necessary that were identified when the event was analyzed were implemented as soon as possible.		
7. The staff was informed of the possible root causes of the event.		
8. Education was provided based on any changes in policies, procedures, and practices.		

Questions that could be asked during a deposition of a case manager or clinical manager include:

- Did the nurse(s) successfully complete an orientation program before being assigned to provide care?

- Was a preceptor used for the orientation, and how long was the orientation?

- Does this nurse and do other staff nurses consistently follow the patient-care policies and procedures?

- What does the most recent performance appraisal demonstrate? If there were areas needing improvement, did you provide the necessary resources and reevaluate the nurse/staff after your intervention?

- Does the patient-care policy involved in this case reflect current accepted practices?

To prevent cases from developing, nurse managers should follow these proactive strategies:

- Ensure that staff adhere to federal, professional, and legal standards of care

- Encourage staff to seek certification in their specialties

- Ensure adequate orientation to their position

- Review the job description with each new staff member

- Conduct fair and realistic performance appraisals

- Review high-risk policies at least annually

- Ensure that patient-care policies reflect current nursing practice, state statutes, laws, and Joint Commission or other accreditation standards

- Provide staff with continuing education, formal sessions, and informal modalities, such as self-learning modules, presentations, and case reviews

- Demonstrate that staff is informed of new policies or other related organization business through attendance or proof of communication

- Ensure good communication between all members of the healthcare team

- Develop audit criteria and routinely audit documentation and make changes as necessary to increase compliance

Legal risks for nurses

The legal risks for nurses are numerous as well. As the frontline providers, they will be held accountable for the state Nurse Practice Acts, national standards of nursing practice, and the care that they provide to their patients. Any nurse in a management position should provide support and guidance to a case manager when an adverse event does occur. The case should be reviewed without bias and punishment—the culture of blame is no longer appropriate, as it does not allow for understanding of how the event happened. Once the event has been thoroughly reviewed, the next step is to develop actions to prevent any similar event from occurring again.

Nurses in an adverse event or potential malpractice case will have to answer questions and undergo reviews similar to those described earlier for nurse managers. They will have to demonstrate professional competency, adequate orientation, training, ongoing clinical education, and compliance with established organization policies. The care provided will be evaluated by professional and state standards and by a nurse expert. In such a case, the best defense will be not only in evidence of competence but, of course, in the documentation.

As a case manager responsible for the nursing care services that will be provided, you need to understand that assignment of patient-care duties, orientation to the case, and documentation of such needs to be accurate.

RNs are not only responsible for all of the care they provide, but also for the care they delegate. A signed home health aide work plan indicates that the care necessary was reviewed and within the standards and protocols of the organization. Unfortunately, however, nurses do not always understand the implications of their signature on what is perceived as "another piece of paper."

Professional-negligence claims against nurses

To meet the definition of professional negligence, a nurse's action must be deemed below the professional standard of care. To prevent claims of professional negligence, identify the high-risk areas for you and your staff and focus on improving nursing care and its documentation. Involve your staff in the review of evidence-based nursing research, revision of policies, and compliance with nursing statutes and standards. In the long run, having done so will increase staff compliance, as will then better understand professional liability and will assist you in the development of a sound documentation system.

Most healthcare facilities have staff development or continuing education staff. Their primary function is to orient new staff and provide inservice education for new equipment and procedures. Nonetheless, as a nurse manager or a case manager, you have a duty to ensure that the orientation is completed and that staff members attend the continuing education. It is everyone's duty to evaluate whether the staff is performing competent care.

Nurse managers should take these lessons to heart:

- Follow through with incompetent staff members by reassigning them to less high-risk cases until retrained.

- Provide retraining so that patient safety is not compromised, or if retraining is not achieved, discharge the employee.

- Always reevaluate any employee you have identified as being at risk or unsatisfactory. Do this in a timely manner (Guido, 2006).

National Practitioner Data Bank

The NPDB issued its annual report in 2005 on the numbers of malpractice payments involving nurses:

"All types of Registered Nurses have been responsible for 5,567 malpractice payments (2.0 percent of all payments) over the history of the NPDB. Non-specialized registered nurses were responsible for 61.9 percent of the payments made for nurses" (NPDB, 2005).

The report also detailed:

- Nonspecialized registered nurses: 61.9% of all payments

- Nurse anesthetists: 20% of nurses' payments

- Nurse midwives: 9.3%

- Nurse practitioners: 8.8%

- Advanced nurse practitioners: 0.2%

Figure 5.2 is a summary of the number of reports submitted and accepted into the NPDB for each professional category.

Figure 5.2   National Practitioner Data Bank (NPDB) summary report

Profession	Medical malpractice reports	Licensure, clinical privileges reports
Clinical nurse specialist	9	0
Home health aide (homemaker)	14	0
Licensed practical/vocational nurse	502	4
Nurse anesthetist	1,109	57
Nurse midwife	619	17
Nurse practitioner	645	26
Nurse's aide	72	0
Registered nurse	3,910	41

Data covers September 1, 1990–May 5, 2007

Source: *www.npdb-hipdb.com/pubs/stats/NPDB_Summary_Report.pdf.*

The reasons for nurse-malpractice payment vary depending on type of professional nurse. The majority of payments for nonspecialized nurses involved monitoring, treatment, and medication events.

The median was $100,000 and the mean was $319,905 for all types of nurses in 2005.

The Healthcare Integrity and Protection Data Bank (HIPDB) has "maintained records of health-related civil judgments, criminal convictions, injunctions, licensing and certification actions, exclusions from Federal and State healthcare programs, and other adjudicated actions since November 22, 1999" (HIPDB, 2002).

When the HIPDB was established, the intent was to combat fraud and abuse in health insurance and healthcare delivery. The goal was to promote quality care.

Figure 5.3 summarizes the number of adverse action reports and civil judgment or criminal conviction reports submitted about organizations from August 21, 1996–January 27, 2007.

Figure 5.3 HIPDB reports on organizations		
Organization	Adverse action report	Judgment or conviction reports
Ambulatory clinic/center	63	2
Ambulatory surgical center	30	0
General/acute-care hospital	85	0
Health center/federally qualified health center/community center	4	2
Home health agency/organization	125	11
Hospice/hospice care provider	4	0
Intermediate care facility for mentally retarded/substance abuse	5	0
Mental health center/community mental health center	17	9
Mental health/substance abuse group/practice	30	8
Nursing facility/skilled nursing facility	1,306	24
Psychiatric hospital	17	0
Rehabilitation hospital	12	0

Source: HIPDB reports on organizations. Accessed June 28, 2007.
www.npdb-hipdb.com/search/pubs/stats/HIPDB_Organization_Subject_Summary_Report.pdf.

References

Austin, S. 2006. "Ladies and gentlemen of the jury, I present . . . the nursing documentation." *Nursing2006* 36(1):56–62.

Brent, N. 2001. *Nurses and the Law: A Guide to Principles and Applications,* 2nd edition. Philadelphia: W. B. Saunders.

Croke, E. 2003. "Nurses, negligence, and malpractice." *American Journal of Nursing* 103(9):54–64.

Dailey, M. Newfield, 2005. "Legal Issues in Home Care: Current Trends, Risk-Reduction Strategies and Opportunities for Improvement." *Home Health Care Management and Practice* 17(2):93–100.

Gorski, L. 2006. "Integrating standards into practice-revised standards for home care infusion: What has changed?" *Home Healthcare Nurse* 24(19):627–631.

Guido, G. 2006. *Legal and Ethical Issues in Nursing.* Upper Saddle River, NJ: Pearson Prentice Hall.

The Joint Commission. 2007. "Sentinel Event Glossary of Terms." Available at *www.jointcommission.org/SentinelEvents/se_glossary.htm.*

"Home health: Court blames nurses, in part, for patient's downhill course." 2007. *Legal Eagle Eye Newsletter for the Nursing Profession* 15(2):6.

"Psych patient threatens to harm family member: Court points to duty to take action." 2005 *Legal Eagle Eye Newsletter for the Nursing Profession* 13(3):3.

Medical Malpractice Law and Strategy. 1999. 16(3):1.

National Practitioner Data Bank. 2005. U.S. Department of Health and Human Services Health Resources and Services Administration. Available at *www.npdb-hipdb.com/pubs/stats/2005_NPDB_Annual_Report.pdf.*

Newfield, J. 2006. "Fall-related injuries." *Home Health Care Management and Practice* 18(2):149–151.

Newfield, J. S. 2005. "Current legal issues in providing wound care in the home." *Home Health Care Management and Practice* 17(3):233–242.

Healthcare Integrity and Protection Data Bank. 2002. Available at *www.npdb-hipdb.com/search/pubs/stats/2002_HIPDB_Annual_Report.pdf*

"Quality Monitoring Using Case Mix and Adverse Event Reports Implementing Outcome-Based Quality Improvement at a Home Health Agency." 2001. Department of Health and Human Services Health Care Financing Administration. Accessed 6/28/07. *www.cmshhs.gov/HomeHealthQualityInits/downloads/HHQIOASISOBQMCaseMix.pdf.*

"Pressure sores: Court case points out importance of nursing documentation." 1997. *Legal Eagle Eye Newsletter for the Nursing Profession* 5(6):1

Rosenthal, K. 2005. "Documenting peripheral IV therapy." Nursing2005 35(7):28.

Showers, J. 2000. "What you need to know about negligence lawsuits." *Nursing2000* 30(2):45–49.

Smith, N. 2007. "Preserve independence with fall prevention strategies." *NursingSpectrum* Jan 29, 2007:16.

Improving your documentation

Learning objectives

After reading this chapter, the learner will be able to:

- Identify common charting errors that increase your liability risk
- Explain the consequences of an incomplete clinical record
- Discuss ways to improve nursing documentation

Recognizing and correcting charting mistakes that increase your liability risks

Chapter 5 discussed nursing negligence and the risks in documentation. To recognize and correct charting errors, you need to put on a legal hat and look for red flags in the medical record. According to Austin, an attorney will look through a clinical record for any evidence that will help prove a case of professional negligence.

Here are a few red flags you should be looking for when auditing your documentation:

- Lack of treatment
- Care that was delayed, substandard, or inappropriate
- No evidence of patient teaching or discharge instructions
- Charting inconsistencies
- Battles between healthcare providers
- Lack of informed consent
- Late entries that are not marked as such
- Any improper alterations in the medical record
- Destruction or missing records (Austin, 2006)

Accurate and complete nursing documentation is essential for demonstrating compliance with standards, delivery of state-of-the-art nursing care, and the ability to communicate effectively with everyone involved in patient care. Therefore, it is important to recognize common charting mistakes and avoid using them in your daily practice.

Eight common charting errors

Charting mistakes can lead to allegations of negligence. The following list describes the eight most common charting mistakes, along with how and why you should avoid them.

Failure to document pertinent health or drug information

Nurses conducting admission assessments are responsible for acquiring all pertinent health data that will influence the plan of care. As silly as this mistake may seem, nursing admission assessments and transfer notes are often left incomplete.

Good history-taking skills are especially important during the initial admission assessment, as the assessment is important to the safety and well-being of the patient. Any health information that is not gathered when taking the history or not documented in the appropriate location on the clinical record can lead to adverse consequences.

To avoid this kind of mistake, ensure that you take thorough histories and focus particularly on patients who cannot communicate effectively, are poor historians, or have dementia. Always document conversations with significant others, the transferring agency, or any other source of information. Provide them with continuing education regarding communication skills needed to ascertain a complete and thorough patient history.

Also ensure that any important health or medication information is documented and communicated to others effectively. Neglecting to communicate an important piece of patient information can leave a nurse open to allegations of negligence. To avoid this, record the information in all of the locations designated by your policies. Also encourage the use of bright labels and other accepted means of communicating the information.

Discharge assessments are equally important and must be done in a responsible and economical manner. When the patient is discharged the clinical record needs to demonstrate that the:

- Discharge planning needs were identified at the time of the comprehensive assessment
- Plan of care includes instructions for timely discharge

- The comprehensive assessment is updated and revised at the time of discharge

- Discharge summary includes the patient's medical and health status at the time of discharge; the patient's physician is aware of the availability of the discharge summary and sent it if he or she requests it. (Zuber, 2004)

Failure to record nursing actions

Here is where the rubber meets the road. There needs to be a way to communicate every nursing action, and nurses must get into the habit of documenting them as close as possible to the time they occur. Unfortunately, charting is left to the end of many nurses' busy days. This is not a good habit, and often difficult to break. Here are some guidelines to follow:

- Record all observations, assessments, and actions on the flow sheet or designated form.

- You must chart as close to the time as possible, even if it is a one- or two-line entry.

- Reduce redundancy and only chart the fact once. You do not need to repeat the same data in more than one place. Just be sure it can be found in the clinical record. If there is redundancy in your documentation system, revise it.

Case study

Failure to record medication given

A 56-year-old female patient went to the emergency room of a hospital in May 1999 with complaints that she was lethargic, disoriented, had slurred speech, and other problems. She had been in an auto accident four days earlier. The patient was prescribed 4 mg of Dilaudid. Two days later—and 54 minutes after taking her last dose of the medication—the patient's heart rate dropped to 20–30 bpm, and she subsequently stopped breathing, which caused irreversible brain damage.

The plaintiff claimed that the Dilaudid dose was inappropriate and had caused the respiratory arrest and brain damage. The plaintiff also claimed that a nurse had failed to record a noon dosage of Dilaudid into the chart and that the nurse had failed to notify a physician when the patient could not be awakened for physical therapy later in the afternoon. A different nurse had failed to wake the patient at midnight and administered more Dilaudid, unaware that the Dilaudid had been given earlier.

The hospital claimed that 4 mg of Dilaudid was an appropriate dose and that failure to document the noon dose was a harmless mistake and the additional dose of the medication was appropriate.

Case study

Failure to record medication given (cont.)

According to the published account, an $8.35 million verdict was returned with a finding of 70% liability against the prescribing doctor and the nurse who did not record the noon administration of Dilaudid.

Source: *NSO Case Study* December 2006

Failure to record medications given

This may seem obvious, but how many times have you reviewed a medication administration record (MAR) and found that the medications in the home do not match the interagency transfer sheet or that the admitting nurse did not record all of the medications found in the home?

Avoid nursing negligence by recording all medications to be taken or discontinued and patient/caregiver education regarding both. Always investigate when you suspect that a medication may have been administered but not recorded, and document your findings

Recording on the wrong chart

Sometimes, a simple mistake of misfiling can lead a nurse to chart on the wrong patient.

Errors in this category include:

- Transcribing medication orders into the wrong patient's chart.

- Writing progress notes without confirming the accuracy of the chart you chose. To prevent this error, look at the external name on the chart and always look at the name stamped or written at the top of the document. And always ensure compliance with the National Patient Safety Goal that refers to proper patient identification prior to procedures and medication administration.

Failure to document a discontinued medication

Nurses are responsible for ensuring safe patient care at all levels. When a medication has been ordered to be discontinued, the change must be appropriately noted according to policy and communicated to the patient, caregiver, and other nurses on the case. Nurses also need to comply with the organization's policies concerning cross-checking the physician orders with the medication reconciliation tool. Doing so can prevent serious complications.

Failure to document drug reactions/changes in patient's condition

The literature on "failure to rescue" points to this potential error. Nurses are responsible for the assessment of a patient's reaction to medication and for the identification of any change in a patient's condition. They must have the skill and knowledge to anticipate the clinical needs of a patient. They must also possess critical-thinking skills to intervene appropriately in any adverse reaction or worsening of the patient's condition. But performing this assessment, identification, and intervention is not enough. Nurses must also document that they have done so.

Improper transcription of orders or transcription of improper orders

The RN can be held liable for transcribing improper doses that led to a patient's injury. The nurse can also be held liable for transcribing and carrying out an order that he or she knows to be inaccurate or suspects to be incorrect.

If the nurse discusses both the order and his or her concerns with physician, then there must be documentation of these conversations. All nurses, regardless of clinical setting, must know the medications or research new medications prior to administration. If a nurse is not familiar with a medication and does not seek supervision or assistance with it, questions of clinical competency and ensuring patient safety will come into play if there is any question of malpractice. The public expects that we will continue to keep our professional skills and knowledge up to date. Falling short of this will put a nurse in a difficult position to defend him/herself.

Writing illegible or incomplete records

Illegible handwriting is no longer tolerated by regulatory and accreditation surveyors. With the goal of improving patient safety, the days of laughing at someone's handwriting are over. All providers who document in the clinical record must ensure that what they have written is readable. Should the clinical record be reviewed, it is essential that the author of the record be able to clearly read it. With the advent of electronic health records (EHR), however, this particular risk problem will fade.

Other common charting flaws

- Blank spaces in chart or flow sheet: A blank space may indicate that you failed to give complete care or fully assess the patient. Follow organization policies regarding the documentation tool in use.

- Incorrect countersignatures: Countersignature of someone else's notations must be done according to organizational policy. Does the policy state that the care must be provided in your presence? Or does the person giving the care have the authority and competency to perform the care, and the countersignature just verifies that it was performed?

- Late entries: There are some situations in which a late entry is acceptable practice (e.g., the chart was unavailable when you needed it, the patient was off the unit, you remembered important information after completing your notation, or you forgot to write notes on a particular clinical record). If you must enter a notation later in the clinical record, be sure to follow the organization's policy for doing so. Some policies will have the author label the entry as "late entry" and indicate the date, time, and reason for the late entry, as well as the date and time the entry should have been made.

- Hasty corrections: When a correction is made, it should be done carefully and within practice standards. Here are some general guidelines for correcting mistakes in the clinical record:

  - Follow the proper procedure for making a late entry

  - Draw a single line through the mistaken entry so that the original entry can still be seen

  - Use the words "mistaken entry" instead of "error" above or next to the single line you drew through the original entry

  - Write your initials and the date and time next to "mistaken entry"

The consequences of an incomplete clinical record

Incomplete records are an invitation to disaster. You must document completely in all areas indicated by organizational policy; nobody wants to review a clinical record in retrospect and see gaps in their documentation. Careful attention and compliance with good charting skills is never a waste of one's time. You can be sure that complete clinical records reflect quality patient care.

An incomplete and inaccurate clinical record leaves an organization and the nurse vulnerable to allegations of negligence. An incomplete clinical record:

- Demonstrates that care was incomplete

- Contains gaps, reflecting poor clinical care

- Demonstrates noncompliance with organization policies

- Is used to support allegations of negligence

- Is used to support allegations of fraud

Failure to document completely can thus lead to regulatory deficiencies and legal consequences. If the documentation is incomplete, contains gaps, and was not consistently completed according to the organization's policies, it can be used to support the allegation that there was poor patient care or, worse, that negligence was involved. If the case goes to court it also allows juries to conclude that the nurse did not collect sufficient data, make good clinical decisions, or implement appropriate interventions in compliance with professional and organizational standards.

Tips to improve your documentation

Here are some concrete suggestions to improve documentation, as well as the rationale for why these guidelines are worthwhile.

Tip #1

Write legibly. The Joint Commission and other regulatory bodies now cite facilities if the medical record cannot be read. The reason is simple: Any illegible entry could be misconstrued and lead to an adverse medical event. Patient safety is the first and foremost concern.

Tip #2

Date and time all entries. Doing so will accurately document all nursing actions and patient responses and ensures that the matter will not be left up to memory. It is defensible and prevents misinterpretation of events when reviewed by others. Avoid charting at the end of the work day. Chart as close as possible to the time the assessment and interventions were conducted.

Tip #3

Every entry must be accounted for. The nurse should sign his or her name and credentials for every entry, even if the entry is one line. This will demonstrate which healthcare provider entered which notation. Never leave spaces between someone else's documentation and signature before you begin your entry in the progress notes.

Tip #4

Do not leave any blank spaces. A line should be drawn through any remaining space on the signature line. This way, someone else cannot enter a statement before the signature. It is a way to prevent forgery. Similarly, if you are using EHRs, never give your login information to anyone.

Tip #5

Use black, permanent ink for entries. Avoid using colored pens, pencils, or felt-tip pens. They do not photocopy well and can be altered.

Tip #6

Do not erase, obliterate, or "white out" any portion of the medical record. To properly correct errors, draw one line through the entry; write "mistaken entry" above it; initial, time, and date the line; and continue to document the correct information on the next available line. Doing so eliminates the suspicion of a cover-up.

Tip #7

Write factual entries. Avoid the dangers associated with giving opinions, assumptions, or meaningless statements (e.g., "Had a good day," "Was drunk and obnoxious"). In addition to being accurate and complete, observations, interventions, and patient responses should use objective data. In this way entries cannot be misinterpreted.

Tip #8

Record entries as close as possible to the care given. A timely entry assists the nurse in documenting events accurately because the facts are fresh and it does not leave the nurse open to questions of reliability.

Tip #9

Review agency policies on a regular basis and adhere to them when documenting in the clinical record. Doing so demonstrates professional accountability and compliance with institution policies, which is key for you and your legal defense.

Tip #10

Follow institution policy when adding omitted information to an already existing entry. For example, your policy might stipulate that you write "late entry" or "addition to nursing note of [Mo/Date/Yr and time]." Following this policy further demonstrates staff compliance with established standards of documentation.

Tip #11

Use only abbreviations adopted by the agency. This demonstrates your adherence to institution policy and to preventing misinterpretation of the entry. It is now a requirement for all healthcare agencies, and following it demonstrates compliance with standards issued by The Joint Commission and other accrediting bodies.

Tip #12

Make sure every clinical record page has the patient's correct name and other identifiers. Doing so eliminates mistaken identification and wrong entries/notations. It also assists in proving that the documentation belongs to the patient when the medical record is photocopied for reimbursement purposes, legal cases, etc.

Tip #13

Be thorough when recording contact with a physician, supervisor, or others (including other staff nurses). Make sure that everyone's contact documentation includes the following information:

- The manner of communication
- The names of those contacted
- What was discussed
- What response took place as a result of the contact
- Any new orders
- The care provided
- Patient's response to the newly ordered care

This gives a historical and accurate accounting of the event, showing that the nurse used the chain of command and was a patient advocate for quality care.

Tip #14

Do not countersign any order, narrative entry, or other documentation unless you can attest to the accuracy of the information. Doing so prevents you from being associated with any potential for liability at a later date.

Tip #15

Make sure that all unusual incidents, such as falls or other types of patient injury, are documented in the record. An incident report is not enough. Be sure that you write in objective, factual terms. Document what was observed, any relevant clinical or other data, interventions, and response to interventions. Do not write "incident report completed." Doing so makes the document accessible if the case goes to litigation.

Tip #16

Whenever a patient leaves the nurse's care (e.g., for a physician office visit), an entry in the medical record should reflect the time, condition of the patient at the last visit, etc. Such an entry proves status of the patient while in a nurse's care.

Tip #17

Information concerning a patient transfer must be in the clinical record. Include:

- Date and time of transfer
- Patient condition when transferred

- Who provided the transfer

- Where and to whom the patient was transferred

- Manner of transfer

Recording these details establishes a baseline and proves the status of the patient while in a nurse's care.

Tip #18

Consent to or refusal of treatment must be documented in the record. It can be any of the following:

- Written consent

- Refusal form

- Documentation in progress notes

This documentation demonstrates informed consent, or that the patient played a role in his or her care plan. Be sure to include critical discussion points to demonstrate that key points were discussed and the level of patient/family understanding.

Tip #19

Patient/family teaching and discharge planning must be documented. This documentation withstands legal challenges to your professional standard of care. Ensure the completeness of documentation, its accuracy, and the patient's/family's ability to understand instructions. Patient/family teaching is mandated by The Joint Commission and federal/state regulations.

Tip #20

Always document the patient's response to:

- Medications

- Treatments

- Patient teaching

- Other interventions

Remember that it is the professional standard of practice to assess and document the patient's response to care provided.

Tip #21

Always use correct spelling, punctuation marks, and grammar. Doing so further demonstrates your, as well as your agency's, commitment to professional standards of documentation.

Tip #22

No nurse should document in the medical record for another person. The only exception is when that practice is a "standard" practice, such as in emergency department nursing. Even so, when documenting for another, the nurse "scribe" must accurately reflect who is providing care and who is documenting the care. *Never* sign another nurse's name in any portion of the record. A clinical record is a legal document and entries are attributed to the person who signs as the provider. Hence, that person is held to the care rendered.

References

Austin, S. 2006. "Ladies and gentlemen of the jury, I present . . . the nursing documentation." *Nursing2006* 30(1):56–62.

Nurses Service Organization. 2007. Case of the Month. Available at *www.nso.com/case/cases_area_index.php?id.*

Zuber, R. 2004. "Compliance with discharge assessment and OASIS requirements." *Home Healthcare Nurse* 22(11):744–745.

Developing a foolproof documentation system

Learning objectives

After reading this chapter, the learner will be able to:

- Evaluate the effectiveness of your current documentation system
- Compare various nursing documentation systems
- Explain how to use regulatory or accreditation standards to develop an audit system
- Identify ways to foolproof a nursing documentation system

Building on the foundation of compliance standards

As we have established throughout this book, nursing documentation is critical for a number of reasons. Nursing documentation is:

- The legal record of patient care
- The only written chronological view of the patient's care
- The primary source for communication among all healthcare providers
- Clinical evidence of the rationale for patient-care decisions
- The primary source of validation and evaluation of the care provided
- The written evidence that supports reimbursement/denial of payment
- Used by regulatory and accrediting surveyors to validate continued licensure and accreditation
- One source of data for clinical research, which is essential in establishing evidence-based practice standards

Because documentation is important for so many reasons, agencies' documentation systems must be consistent, effective, and foolproof. This chapter will discuss possible documentation systems and the necessary steps in developing one that is sound. Keep in mind that regardless of the system you choose—paper or electronic—you must comply with regulatory and nursing standards of documentation.

Using the existing federal instruments employed during a survey is the easiest way to build your documentation system and evaluate compliance during clinical record audits. The Department of Health and Human Services'/Centers for Medicare & Medicaid Services' (CMS') forms are on their Web sites for you to review (*www.cms.hhs.gov*/CMSForms/CMSForms/*list.asp*). The Home Health Functional Assessment Instrument used by the surveyors has Modules A–F. Every case manager and other professional staff members need to be familiar with what is being evaluated in his or her documentation and during home visits during the survey. See Figure A.2 and Figure A.5 in the appendix for a sample tool that can be used as an audit tool to evaluate the staff and their compliance with the federal requirements.

Evaluating your current documentation system

As a progressive case manager, you have decided that you want to improve your patient's care by improving the documentation of nursing observations. You also want to reduce the time it takes to document the nursing process. But before you decide to make a recommendation to revise a form or two, take a moment to read the seven items below. Can you concur with all of the following statements?

- Our clinical and patient-satisfaction outcomes speak for themselves. For example, assessment and management of pain is well documented in the medical record and cited in the patient-satisfaction survey as 90+.

- When I have to investigate an adverse event, the documentation gives me all of the information I need to draw my conclusions and take action, if warranted (i.e., standards, policies, etc., were followed).

- At any point in the patient's care, I can find evidence of documented progress or appropriate interventions to improve the patient's care.

- When I review a specific clinical record I can see that I used the nursing process.

- There is clear communication and collaboration evident in the clinical record (e.g., conversations, consultations, communication among team members).

- Discharge planning is clearly documented at the onset, frequently (according to agency policy), and not left to the day of discharge.

- When the clinical records are audited as part of ongoing performance improvement, the compliance rate is 95%–100% (or your target rate).

If you agree with each of these statements, you probably don't need to change much. If you disagree with any of these, you may need to think about seriously looking at your documentation system in an effort to improve patient safety and outcomes.

In any healthcare agency today, you will find numerous documentation forms—or screens, if electronic—based on history and what someone thought was needed for the regulatory and accrediting agencies. You may also find an inconvenient system that produces data redundancy, inconsistency, and irregularity of charting. The forms or formats may be too long, repetitious, and time-consuming. In fact the forms may not even reflect the amount of nursing care provided and do not facilitate communication of family needs. Based on the acuity and staffing of today's nursing world, you need to take a hard look at any documentation system that is descriptive in style, as it is inappropriate for the current workload of today's busy nurses (Cheevakasemsook, 2006).

Your success with improving nursing documentation will be based on several components, such as current documentation policy, your administration's support, and the organizational culture. To improve documentation, you will need to be involved and function as a positive facilitator. You can develop a short-term quality improvement project team or delegate chart auditing to the staff. There are many ways to accomplish this goal.

Systems of documentation

There are various well-established systems of documentation to consider for your organization. The following are brief summaries of the various systems to introduce what is currently available to you and your staff. Keep in mind that regardless of the system you implement, it will only be as successful as you want it to be. Change is, at times, difficult for the staff, but your ability to manage change, use performance improvement processes, and monitor proper use of the documentation system will contribute to your success. The following systems can also be used in the electronic health record when nurses address variances in the patient's response to the plan of care.

Problem-oriented medical record (POMR)

The POMR system forces the nurse to think in a "problem-oriented" manner and organizes information so that every aspect of the patient's status and care is evident. It lends itself nicely to nursing, as it mirrors the nursing process.

You may recognize this system: It uses the SOAP format for narrative documentation. In this format, subjective (S) and objective (O) data is documented and analyzed. The provider's assessment (A) is also documented and gives the reviewer an understanding of how the provider made decisions. The plan (P) of care is also documented, which explains why, what, and how the provider dealt with the patient's healthcare needs.

In the original design, the problem-oriented charting had the following components: database, problem list, initial plan, progress notes, and discharge summary. Some organizations no longer use a problem list, but that is a decision you and the staff will have to make, because ongoing updating is necessary when you use a "problem list."

In its evolution, the SOAP format has changed to include any interventions (I), evaluation (E), and revision (R), or changes to the original plan. These could be changes to the intervention, outcome of care, or timeline. There are advantages to using this format for all narrative notes: It helps the nursing staff think through the nursing process and document it in a recognizable format (SOAPIE). Refer to the example in Figure 7.1.

| Figure 7.1 | POMR example |

7/14/07 1100

S: "I don't like using that thing."

O: Patient has not been using the blood glucose monitor for three days. Current blood sugar level is 60 with no signs/symptoms of hypoglycemia. Discussed the importance of maintaining blood sugar levels within range as well as of the blood glucose monitor.

A: Ineffective health maintenance R/T ineffective coping.

P: Continue to assess patient's reasons for not following prescribed plan care. Monitor for s/s of low blood sugar.

I: Reinforce teaching using visual aids and demonstration techniques. Recognize resistance to change in lifelong patterns of daily care and discuss ways to accommodate this new plan of care. Validate the patient's feelings regarding the impact of his health status on his current lifestyle.

E: Patient verbalized understanding and demonstrated correct use of the monitor.

The POMR system has been modified and is sometimes referred to as a problem-oriented record (POR). This system is used by hospitals, nursing homes, and home health agencies.

The components of this system are similar to the POMR, as it also uses a database, problem list, initial plan, and progress notes. The progress notes use charting based on the SOAP, SOAPIE, or SOAPIER format (Daniels, 2004).

Problem-Intervention-Evaluation (PIE) system

The goal of PIE system charting is to eliminate the traditional patient care plan and incorporate it as an ongoing plan of care into the daily nursing documentation. Like the POMR system, this documentation format uses the nursing process as its basis.

Using the PIE format ensures that your staff members document their nursing diagnoses, interventions related to the nursing diagnosis, and their evaluation of the care rendered. This format has two major documentation tools: a daily assessment sheet and nursing progress notes. The daily assessment sheet includes major categories, such as respirations, routine care, and monitoring. It will also include space to record pertinent treatment. Any abnormal findings are identified by an asterisk, and the detailed information is documented in the nursing progress notes.

The system includes the problem (P) the patient presents and the nursing diagnosis. The staff should use either the list of accepted nursing diagnoses from the North American Nursing Diagnosis Association (NANDA) or your facility-approved nursing diagnoses. Your written guidelines should also allow the nurse to use a problem statement if the approved nursing diagnosis does not correlate to the patient's condition. The nurse must document all of the nursing diagnoses/patient problems in the nursing progress notes. Each is labeled as "P" with a corresponding number, such as "P#1."

The interventions (I) or implementation of the planned actions should use the same format as the problem. The intervention is identified with the corresponding number to the nursing diagnosis/problem (e.g., IP#1). The "E" represents the evaluation of the care given. After the nurse charts his or her interventions and then the related patient response, he or she performs an evaluation (E) of the care given and documents it with "E," followed by the assigned problem number, (e.g., "EP#1"). See Figure 7.2.

Figure 7.2	Example of nursing progress notes using PIE	
7/31/07	0800	P#2: Pain related to postop status._____
		IP#2: Pain identified as 10 out of 10. Grimacing with movement—see pain assessment for other descriptors. Reviewed MD orders and encouraged patient to self-medicate with Percocet.
		Reassess pain level at 0830. Continue to assess pain with each visit.
		._____
	0830	EP#2: Pain identified as 4 out of 10._____ P. Smith, RN

Focus charting

The focus charting method assists the nurse in organizing the narrative nursing notes to include data, action, and response for each identified patient concern. According to Smith, focus charting helps the staff monitor patient problems and avoid repetitious documentation. A "focus" may be written as a nursing diagnosis, a change in condition or a potential problem, or a treatment/procedure or a patient behavior (Smith, 2000).

The use of the key word "focus" to describe the patient concern eliminates the negative connotation of the word "problem." Focus charting encourages the use of assessment data to evaluate the patient-care area of concern.

This format of documentation is similar to the SOAP format, using letters to assist the nurse in his or her documentation of patient care. Introduced by a committee of staff nurses in the early 1980s as a way to streamline the documentation process, it uses patient-centered identified concerns as the focus of an entry.

Data (D), action (A), and response (R) are used in this system. As in SOAP, data should include subjective and objective information. The action should include a statement related to current and future nursing interventions, as well as the changes in the plan of care due to the nurse's assessment findings. The response should include the patient's reaction to the nursing (or any other member of the patient-care team) interventions (see Figure 7.3). Some agencies add P (plan) to their focus-charting format.

Figure 7.3 **Example of focus charting**

Date	Time	Focus	Nursing progress notes
7/21/07	0100	Altered mental status	D: HH aide reported patient had period of one minute staring. Upon arrival patient confused as to time and place. See neuro assessment. A: Physician notified of findings. Continue to monitor patient for mental status changes. Change fall risk plan of care. HH aide and spouse instructed in safety measures. P. Smith, RN
7/21/07	0200		R: Returned to baseline at the end of visit. P. Smith, RN

'AIR' charting

This charting format, which should be used in conjunction with flow sheets and patient-care plans, is another way to keep the narrative documentation simple and organized. It assists the nurse in avoiding repetition of information that can be found elsewhere in the medical record.

The assessment (A) represents the nurse's physical-assessment findings. Documentation will begin by titling each specific issue—a nursing diagnosis, admission note, or discharge plan—that the nurse addresses. The interventions (I) are the summary of the nursing actions (and those of others on the healthcare team) taken in response to the assessment data. It may be a shortened version of the patient's plan of care, including the need for additional patient monitoring, if warranted.

The "R" is the response of the patient (or patient outcome) to the nursing interventions. Because it may not be evident at the time of the documentation, the response might not be included until later. In fact, the response may be documented by another nurse. Keep in mind that the key to the success of this format is the notation of each of the nurse's assessments and interventions.

Charting by exception (CBE)

CBE, or variance charting, is a system for documenting exceptions to a disease progression. If you implement the CBE system, you must also have the most up-to-date and comprehensive patient-care standards in place. They will need to be clear and specific as to the exceptions and what the staff is expected to document (see Figure 7.4). In addition, as part of the CBE, you will need several types of flow sheets, up-to-date protocols and incidental orders, nursing databases, nursing diagnosis–based care plans, and SOAP format for nursing progress notes (Iyer, 1999).

Figure 7.4	**Example of CBE assessment standards**	
Assessments	**Components**	**Expected outcomes**
Cardiovascular	Apical rate, heart rhythm, blood pressure, edema (periorbital, sacral, pedal, and generalized), palpitations, calf tenderness, presence of jugular vein distension.	Apical rate and BP are within patient's normal limits and in comparison to patient's baseline. Rhythm is regular. No edema, calf tenderness, or palpitations. Absence of JVD. Absence of chest pain with activity.

This example is adapted from Marelli, T. 1997. *Nurse Manager's Survival Guide.* St. Louis: Mosby.

Key elements in CBE include:

- Flow sheets, such as graphic record, fluid balance record, daily nursing assessments record, skin assessment, client teaching, and discharge record.

- Standards of nursing care. This can be accomplished by referencing the agency's printed standards of nursing practice. You will need to identify minimum criteria for your patients regardless of the clinical area.

- Bedside access to the medical record forms. All flow sheets must be kept at the patient's bedside to allow for timely documentation. Also think about including "N/A" on your flow sheets to avoid the possible misinterpretation that the assessment or intervention was not done (Berman, 2008).

If you consider using this format, you will need to be sure that your charting policies do not conflict with state and federal regulations or those of The Joint Commission. Have your risk manager, agency attorney, interdisciplinary committees, and regulatory manager review and approve any CBE plans (Smith, 2002).

Patient-care plans

The patient care plan (485) is not a stand alone documentation system; it is the legal record of the patient's home health plan of care. It is a necessary and required part of home healthcare documentation. The plan of care is the primary means of communication between the physician and other team members. Beyond this, it should be seen as much more than just the plan of care. According to Siegler, the 485 should be:

- A teaching and quality improvement tool

- A communication tool with information for the physician about how to maximize a safe transition to the home

- A prompt to physicians and nurses to follow evidence-based guidelines for chronic illnesses such as heart failure and diabetes

- A way of encouraging a physician to develop a plan of care based on diagnoses, functional status, and goals

- A tool to promote cost-effective, creative utilization of skilled services to maximize patient function and prevent readmission to the hospital

- Easy to read, guiding the physician to review the data before signing (Siegler, 2006)

The staff at Weill Medical College of Cornell University and the Visiting Nurse Service of New York conducted a joint project to redesign the electronic 485. The outcome was a more physician-friendly version that just reordered the following clinical content:

1. Patient diagnoses

2. Patient allergies

3. Patient functional limitations

4. Patient mental status

5. Patient prognosis

6. Patient goals

7. Home care orders (including medications)

8. Home care discharge plan

To review a revised electronic 485 go to *www.vnsny.org/research/projects/Fig1_Prototype485.pdf* (Siegler, 2006).

The patient care plan should be able to be used by an agency nurse who may not know the patient or his or her needs. There can be some standardization, but staff will be constantly reminded that each care plan must reflect the specific patient care needs.

Clinical pathways

Also referred to as *critical pathways, care maps, care paths,* or *multidisciplinary action plans,* clinical pathways define the optimal sequence and timing of specific interventions for specific diagnoses or procedures. The format encourages interdisciplinary collaboration by clearly setting expectations for the patient's outcome for all the disciplines involved in delivering care to the patient.

Everyone on the team is expected to work toward measurable outcomes within the prescribed length of time. The pathways should always be built on evidence-based standards of medical and nursing care—they are to be used as guidelines and not as substitutes for sound nursing judgment. There are many examples and preexisting pathways that can help the healthcare team identify, measure, and analyze the patient's care and outcomes. They can focus on the patient's clinical problems, phases of care, or diagnoses. Keep in mind, although it may appear to be a standardized approach to care, this tool should allow each discipline the ability to individualize it based on the patient's status.

This format lends itself to varying levels of use. Some organizations use it as their whole documentation system, with various documentation tools to supplement each pathway. Other organizations have used it to decrease practice variation among the healthcare team members. That is a great advantage of this system—it can be used in all levels of the healthcare continuum (e.g., outpatient centers, hospitals, home health agencies, and long-term care facilities). It also ensures patient education, continuity of care among team members, continuity of information, improved quality of patient care, reduced length of stay, and reduced cost of care (Renholm, 2002).

Outcome-based charting

The primary focus of this documentation system is patient behavior following a nurse's intervention. It is built on identification of the patient's problem and formulation of patient outcomes on the patient-care plan, which are based on both subjective and objective data. The evaluation process continues until discharge.

This documentation system has three components—a database, a patient plan of care, and expected-outcome statements. The database includes subjective and objective data used to identify the patient's problems and educational needs. The plan of care is developed from this initial database, and it should include expected outcomes and related nursing interventions. Examples of patient-care plans that include expected outcomes are:

- Clinical pathways or care maps

- Standardized care plans

- Patient-care guidelines

- Traditional handwritten care plans

The expected-outcome statements, also known as *goals* or *objectives*, are derived from the patient's nursing diagnoses. These statements must be specific and focused on the patient's behavior. Always encourage the patient/family to participate in the development of the outcomes (Weinstock, 1999). An example of expected outcomes and outcome criteria appears in Figure 7.5.

Figure 7.5   Example of outcome criteria

Nursing diagnosis	Expected outcome	Outcome criteria
Pain related to postop	Pain will be minimized within 24 hours	• Pain will be relieved, as described by patient, to a level of 3 or less out of 10 • Patient will be able to increase ambulation from assist of one to independent

'FACT' system

This documentation system incorporates many of the charting-by-exception principles. Designed to avoid documentation of irrelevant data, decrease repetitive nursing notes, and reduce documentation time, this format requires nurses to only document exceptions to the norm. The "FACT" system has the following four components:

F   Flow sheets, which are individualized to specific services.

A   Assessment, the aspects of which are standardized within baseline parameters.

C   Concise, integrated progress notes and flow sheets that document the patient's condition and responses.

T   Timely entries. Care is recorded when it is given.

This system requires specific documentation forms—initial assessment such as the OASIS, also an assessment-action flow sheet, a frequent-assessment flow sheet such as skilled visit notes, and narrative progress notes. The initial assessment is used as the baseline assessment; progress notes (that use the date, action, response [DAR] format) and flow sheets document the ongoing assessment of the patient.

Flow sheets

The flow sheet allows for timely and rapid documentation at the time of assessment and intervention in a concise and chronological format. If used correctly, a flow sheet gives the reviewer a picture of the patient's clinical course. It also contains valuable objective data that all healthcare team members can use to assess the patient's progress. However, the issue with flow sheets is when a nurse does not fill in all aspects of a sheet. Any documentation tool you have is vulnerable to the whims of the user. Always ensure complete and accurate charting by completing every box on the form or screen.

Flow sheets are to be used in conjunction with narrative notes. Unless you build into the flow sheet adequate space for comments, narrative notes will document subjective data, detailed interventions, and unusual incidents.

Narrative charting

This remains a predominant method of nursing documentation. Left to their own devices, nurses do not focus on the aspects of documentation required for the promotion of quality patient care and averting legal pitfalls. Without continuing education, audits, and ongoing feedback, nurses will write lengthy notes repeating what is on the flow sheet and make insignificant notations just to fill the space. There will not be a focus on the necessary components for home health care, such as addressing the admission problem, home-bound status, general problems assessed, and progress toward goals/outcomes. Nurses also have difficulty documenting variances—staying focused on the clinical changes assessed, what interventions were implemented, the patient's response to those interventions, and any patient education conducted.

Narrative progress notes are not asking for a novel—nursing documentation must be concise, complete, and accurate. If the information can be found in another section of the medical record or on another form of documentation, you do not need to repeat it.

When developing an audit tool be sure and include a way to measure the staff's use of the nursing process in their progress notes. Look for nursing diagnoses, written assessment, evidence of care planning, implementation of nursing interventions, and assessment of the patient's response to the nursing interventions. Remember, any time spent on audits will help to evaluate your staff's compliance with agency documentation protocols and how well they have developed critical-thinking skills (Berman, 2008). See Figure 7.6 for an example of an audit tool.

| Figure 7.6 | Audit tool to evaluate nursing process |

MR #: _____ Nurse: _____

Date audit done: _____ Date of audited notes: _____

Documented Item	Yes	No	Comments
Appropriate nursing diagnosis used			
Assessment data was relevant (to nursing diagnosis)			
Evidence of care planning			
Appropriate nursing interventions			
Demonstrated evaluation of nursing interventions			
Evidence of client's response to nursing interventions			

Encouraging the use of the nursing process and accurate documentation of that process is a win-win situation:

- For the patient, it provides a scientific approach in which the nurse can render care

- For you, it provides a way to measure compliance with nursing standards of practice

- For the organization, it may avert allegations of negligence, as the documentation will demonstrate a methodical approach to thinking, providing patient care, and documenting that process

Figure 7.7 provides an overview of which documentation systems are applicable in different settings.

| | Figure 7.7 | Comparison of charting systems |
| | | |

	Acute care	Ambulatory care	Home health care	LTC	Mental health facilities	Rehabilitation facilities
Format						
AIR	X			X		
CBE	X			X		
Computerized	X	X	X	X	X	X
Core	X			X		
FACT	X		X	X		
Focus/DAR	X		X	X	X	X
Outcome-based	X		X	X	X	X
PIE	X		X			
POMR	X		X	X	X	X

Using the Joint Commission standards as the foundation of your system

When you decide to revise your documentation system, you must make sure that regulatory and accrediting standards are self-evident in the new system. One reason is that the new Joint Commission survey process will rely on the medical record more so than in the past.

Under the new survey process, called *tracer methodology*, a patient's course and provision of care will need to be reflected in his or her medical record. Therefore, review the Joint Commission standards and identify the components of documentation that you and your project team will need to include. In fact, you can use the Joint Commission standards and language to compose your new documentation tool—the expected documentation components are clearly spelled out in the accreditation manual.

Figure 7.8 is a small sample of what The Joint Commission surveyors will now evaluate in relation to what should be documented. The tool was based on the 2007 home healthcare requirements for patient-specific data.

Figure 7.8	**Nursing medical record audit**
	(based on the Joint Commission standards)

[Name of] Hospital
NURSING MEDICAL RECORD AUDIT
The Joint Commission Standards

Unit: _____ Patient initials/age: _____ MR #: _____

Date of audit: _____ Auditor: _____

EoP	General items	Met	Not met	N/A	Comments
RI.2.40 EP 3	A complete informed consent process				
RI.2.80 EP 4	Documentation of whether or not the patient has signed an advance directive.				
RI.2.80 EP 9	Documentation indicating hospital followed patient's wishes re: organ donation				
IM.6.20 EP 2	Nursing documents contain demographic information: • Pt's name, sex, address, date of birth, and authorized representative • Legal status of patients receiving behavioral health care services • Pt's language and communication needs				
EOP	**Assessment of patients**	**Met**	**Not met**	**N/A**	**Comments**
PC.2.20 EP 4	Initial assessment includes: • Physical assessment • Psychological assessment • Social assessment • Nutrition and hydration status • Functional status End-of-life care includes: • Social variables • Spiritual variables • Cultural variables				

Figure 7.8	Nursing medical record audit (cont.)				
EoP	Assessment of patients (cont.)	Met	Not met	N/A	Comments
PC.2.120 EP 3	Nursing assessment is completed w/in 24 hrs of inpatient admission				
PC.2.120 EP 5	Nutritional screening (if applicable) completed w/in 24 hrs of inpatient admission				
PC.2.120 EP 5	Functional status screening (if applicable) w/in 24 hrs of inpatient admission				
PC.2.150 EP 1	There is documentation of patient being reassessed per hospital policy				
PC.3.230 EP 1	Diagnostic testing and procedures are performed as ordered				
PC.4.10 EP 1	Documentation demonstrates that the care, treatment, and services are individualized				
PC.4.10 EP 2	Patient plan of care based on data from assessments				
PC.8.10 EP 1	Documentation of comprehensive pain assessment				
PC.8.10 EP 3	Documentation of reassessment per hospital policy				*See above PC.2.150 EP1*
PC.12.40 PC.12.40 EP 1 PC.12.40 EP 4 PC.12.40 EP 5	Initial assessment of patient who is at risk for harming self or others, identifies: • Techniques, methods, or tools used to control patient behavior • Identification of preexisting medical conditions or physical disabilities that place the patient at greater risk during restraint or seclusion • Any hx of physical or sexual abuse				
PC.15.20 EP 2	Documentation of patients being informed of plan for D/C or transfer to another organization or level of care				

Figure 7.8	Nursing medical record audit (cont.)				
EoP	**Documentation of care of patients**	**Met**	**Not met**	**N/A**	**Comments**
PC.4.10 EP 12	Documentation of evaluation of patient related to patient care goals				
PC.4.10 EP 13	Documentation of revised goals of care, treatment, and services				
PC.4.10 EP 15	Documentation of revised plan of care, treatment, and services based on patient status				
PC.8.70 EP 1	When appropriate, documentation of patient/family needs and nursing interventions related to: • Comfort • Dignity • Psychosocial needs • Emotional needs • Spiritual needs • Death and grief				
MM.6.10 EP 2	Documentation of medication effects includes: • Patient's perception of efficacy • Use of info from pt's medical record (lab results, clinical response, medication profile)				
IM.6.10 EP 4	Nursing care entries are dated, author identified and authenticated per hospital policy				
IM.6.50 EP 2	Verbal or telephone orders are dated and identify names of individuals who gave, rec'd, and implemented the order				
NPSG 2A	Verbal/telephone orders are "read back" and documented per hospital policy				

Figure 7.8	Nursing medical record audit (cont.)				
EoP	Education	Met	Not met	N/A	Comments
PC.6.10 EP 2	Documentation of assessment of learning needs: • Cultural beliefs • Religious beliefs • Emotional barriers • Desire and motivation to learn • Physical limitations • Cognitive limitations • Barriers to communication process				
PC.6.10 EP 3	Documentation of patient education of the following: • Plan for care, treatment • Basic health practices and safety • Safe and effective use of medications • Nutrition interventions, modified diets or oral health • Safe and effective use of medication equipment or independence possible • Supplies if provided by hospital • Understanding pain, risk for pain, importance of effective pain management, pain assessment process, and methods for pain management • Rehab techniques to help them reach maximum				
PC.6.30 EP 2	Education is coordinated among disciplines involved in care, treatment, and services				
PC.6.30 EP 5	Documentation of patient comprehension				

Figure 7.8	Nursing medical record audit (cont.)				
EoP	**Education (cont.)**	**Met**	**Not met**	**N/A**	**Comments**
PC.6.50 EP 2	Pediatric patients: hospital addresses academic educational needs				
PC.15.20 EP 7	Pt. is educated about how to obtain further care, treatment, and services to meet identified needs				
EoP	**Discharge information**	**Met**	**Not met**	**N/A**	**Comments**
PC.15.20 EP 8	Documentation of arrangement or assistance for services needed to meet patient needs after discharge				
PC.15.20 EP 9	Documentation of written, understandable D/C instructions				
PC.15.30 EP 1	Documentation of appropriate information to any organization or provider to which patient is transferred or D/C'd				
IM.6.10 EP 7	Discharge summary includes: • Reason for hospitalization • Significant findings • Procedures performed and care, treatment, and services provided • Patient's condition at D/C • Information given to patient/family				

Other regulatory documentation requirements should also be incorporated into your documentation. Remember, there is no perfect documentation system or form. If you are a clinical manager, you simply need to ensure that you have worked toward the development of the best documentation system possible for your agency, using all of the evidence-based nursing standards and regulatory and accreditation requirements. Then, your next step will be to ensure compliance with all aspects of the medical record through continuous monitoring.

Ten steps for ensuring a foolproof documentation system

Working on the development or revision of a foolproof documentation system is similar to building an audit system—you must review all of the regulatory, accreditation, and organizational standards in preparation. In addition, the project team will have to include all levels of staff. The professional staff should include nursing, nursing management, risk management, quality (or the Joint Commission coordinator), social work services, and any other discipline that could be involved in the review and reconstruction of the documentation system. Keep in mind that the goal is to build a complete but concise documentation system. In doing so, you will have to evaluate all existing forms/tools to determine their current level of compliance with standards and redundancy across the disciplines.

- **Step 1:** Review all of the standards and evidence-based nursing practice. This may seem like an overwhelming task, but it is necessary in ensuring that the final product contains the elements necessary to meet compliance with all required standards (e.g., state, federal, Joint Commission). This research phase is a great time to involve staff. It exposes them to contemporary nursing practice and opens the lines of communication regarding why change is necessary.

  Once you have your project team in place, this first step can be divided. One or two people who are familiar with their own required standards should review the current state, federal, and Joint Commission standards. In fact, the existing documentation tool should be graded as to whether it meets each documentation-related element in a Joint Commission standard (e.g., using a notation in the margin of the page next to each standard). Other members of the project team can review nursing literature for related nursing research and professional standards. In reviewing compliance with the standards, the team can identify the weaknesses in the existing documentation tool. From this self-evaluation, you can progress to Step 2.

- **Step 2:** Build the documentation system and the respective tools based on actual language written by the accrediting body (The Joint Commission or CHAP). Incorporate state and federal standards when the Joint Commission standards do not apply.

- **Step 3:** In collaboration with the project team, construct a matrix for each of the disciplines and its required standards. In doing so, you will see whether there is any redundancy in patient information that can be captured in one area or by one discipline. Once again, the goal is to streamline the documentation system while ensuring documentation of the required standards. If your documentation system duplicates efforts or if it is not easy to use, it will not be used to the fullest extent by the staff.

- **Step 4:** Cut and paste, if using a paper system. That is, cut the section(s) of the existing tool(s) that do not require changes and paste them into what will become the new tool. Not only is this a simple way to revise documentation, but it is also a fast and effective way to ensure that some of the existing documentation tool is included in the revision. If the revised tool is similar in appearance, content, or form, the staff is less likely to resist the changes. Education also becomes easier because unchanged sections will be a welcome relief for the staff member who has to complete the new form under the pressures of a busy day.

- **Step 5:** Once the documentation tool is complete, send it to the print shop or graphics department for a proof. Review the tool and confirm that all of the elements required in the standards are apparent.

- **Step 6:** Post the proposed documentation tool so that all may review and comment. Many times, the project team may not see the obvious. Creating a "review and comment" period assists you in promoting future buy-in and decreases the likelihood of an oversight reaching the final version.

- **Step 7:** Write documentation guidelines for every documentation tool in your organization. They assist in the education on how the tool is to be used. If you are in a multisystem organization, the guidelines ensure that all facilities in the organization are informed of how the documentation tool is to be used.

  Documentation guidelines can be used whenever you have a new employee or a nurse needing reeducation. Include the guidelines as part of orientation/education in a self-study packet, rather than giving a formal class on all of the documentation tools the employee is expected to complete.

  Documentation guidelines also encourage compliance with the documentation tool. The nurse manager can use them as a means of communicating expected compliance with a staff member who is not accurately completing the document.

  If the clinical record is under review (e.g., by a surveyor), they will demonstrate that, in fact, the documentation tool in question was completed according to established guidelines.

- **Step 8:** If there is resistance to using the new documentation tool, bargain with the staff. Although there may have been staff representation on the project team, everyone might not be ready for the changes proposed. Convince staff members that the changes are necessary to comply with evidence-based nursing practice and regulatory or accrediting standards. Ask them to try the new/revised documentation tool for 90 days—it takes that long for the staff members to become acclimated to the tool. Then ask them to give constructive feedback as to what is working and what is not.

- **Step 9:** Audit, audit, audit. The key to successful implementation and continuing staff compliance is an audit system. The staff members will want constructive feedback from the auditors, and they will welcome the opportunity to perfect the documentation system, as doing so will assist them in their busy day.

  Be sure to post the audit results—make them visually appealing and understandable. Use them as part of your ongoing performance-improvement plan for your department or unit. Given the legal, financial, and regulatory ramifications, accurate and complete documentation is a must, and the goal should be no less than 100% compliance.

- **Step 10:** Celebrate success. Whenever you have an opportunity to promote the success of your staff, do so. It builds self-confidence, moves the unit toward a "center of excellence," and makes it a model for other units.

References

Berman, A. 2008. *Fundamentals of Nursing: Concepts, Process, and Practice.* Upper Saddle River, NJ: Pearson.

Cheevakasemsook, A. 2006. "The study of nursing documentation complexities." *International Journal of Nursing Practice* 12(6):366–374.

Daniels, R. 2004. *Nursing Fundamentals: Caring and Clinical Decision Making.* Clifton Park, NY: Delmar Learning.

Iyer, P. 1999. *Nursing Documentation: A Nursing Process Approach,* 3rd edition. Philadelphia: Mosby.

Renholm, M. 2002. "Critical pathways: A systematic review" *JONA* 32(4):196–201.

Siegler, E. 2006. "Improving the transition to home healthcare by rethinking the purpose and structure of the CMS 485: First steps." *Home Health Care Services Quarterly* 25(3/4):27–38.

Smith, L. 2002. "How to chart by exception." *Nursing2002* 32(9):30.

Smith, L. 2000. "How to use focus charting." *Nursing2000* 30(5):76.

Weinstock, D. 1999. *Mastering Documentation,* 2nd edition. Springhouse, PA: Springhouse.

Auditing your documentation system

Learning objectives

After reading this chapter, the learner will be able to:

- Identify the advantages of a strong documentation audit system
- Develop an audit system based on performance-improvement goals
- Identify strategies for the implementation of audits by staff members
- Identify tips to help clinical supervisors implement an effective audit system

The important role audits play in protecting you and your organization

There is nothing more loathsome than conducting chart audits. They are tedious and boring, and nothing is ever done with the results, right? Wrong! Once you have set your sights on what you want to accomplish related to patient care outcomes and documentation, an audit will give you the data to celebrate success. If you have not achieved your target, then the data identify the reasons the documentation tool or system is not working. In the end, auditing is the key to quality patient care, reduction of legal risks, and compliance with standards.

Building your audit system around performance improvement goals

In the beginning of the book, we emphasized the attributes of the nursing process as a systematic approach to providing comprehensive patient care. The same applies to the development and use of an audit system.

Begin with a performance improvement (PI) process that you understand and are most comfortable with. You may be familiar with the PDSA (plan, do, study, act) cycle, for example. I also became familiar with Dr. Juran's comprehensive approach to planning, setting, and reaching goals. Because the steps in this PI process are similar to those in the nursing process, they help staff understand why audits are important and why there may be areas that still need improvement.

The PI process—PI cycle—is like the nursing process. It is cyclical—each step is well-defined and builds and moves you and your team forward to the next (see Figure 8.1).

Figure 8.1 **Steps in the quality improvement process**

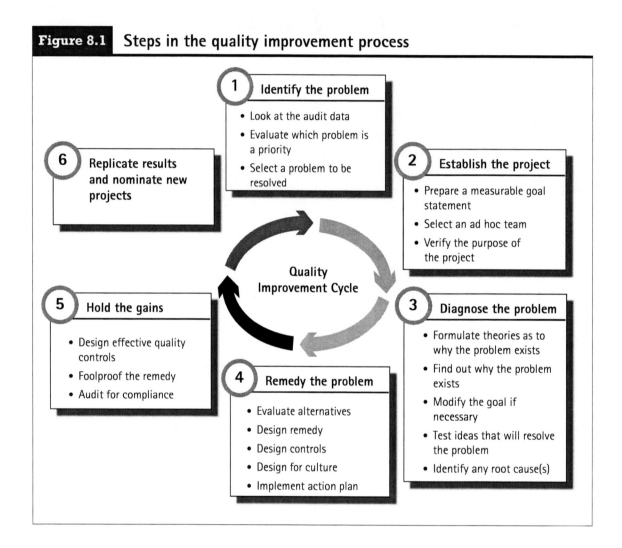

The goal of each step is to find the root cause of the system or process failure. Once the root cause is found, the remedies can be developed and implemented.

In healthcare, we often implement a new process or revise an old process to improve documentation. This type of improvement may only last through its initial phase—how compliant is the staff one year after the change? The education may have been provided and completed; the staff may have been excited about the new documentation tool, but the downfall of every changed process is a lack of monitoring. Six months from the rollout of a new tool, your random reviews could reveal a flaw, gap, or worse yet, an incident could occur and you could have to go back and look at your documentation system. The reasons for audits are clear. You need to:

- Ensure that the system you have designed is an effective quality-control process

- Ensure that your remedy (in this case your documentation tool) is foolproof

- Sustain the success that you and your staff are trying to achieve

Therefore, develop a system for auditing the controls (of the outcome of the documentation system). Decide the following:

- What is being measured?

- What aspects should be reported?

- How often do you audit?

- Where should you report the audit results?

- How often are you going to report the results?

- Who is responsible for monitoring the audit results and giving feedback?

Once you have determined the system for reporting audit results, you can use various tools to display them. Some commonly used data tools include control charts, control spreadsheets, graphs (bar), charts (run, pie), Pareto diagrams, and so on. Ask your quality improvement manager to help you with your visual data tools.

Measuring compliance and improvement through an audit

Audit results can be used to monitor compliance with all of the elements needed in the medical record—standards, quality goals, reimbursement, and so on. The audit results will also give you information (data) on areas you need to improve. You may want to develop a comprehensive tool as the first step in improving your staff's documentation. It must include all of the elements required in your organization, and it should be based on state, federal, Joint Commission, and other quality/risk-management elements.

When creating your first audit tool, you may want to speak with the person in charge of medical records. He or she may have already developed a good model—all you will need to do is change the audit elements. In addition, the manager of medical records has a wealth of resources and may be able to find, for your review, a tool already in place at another organization. Your mantra should be "Do not reinvent the wheel."

Example

Creating a compliance audit tool

Creating a compliance audit tool is easy. I usually start with what I am trying to accomplish. Is it meeting *Conditions of Participation (CoP)*, Joint Commission, or CHAP compliance? The clinical record needs to demonstrate that in fact it is in compliance and that the services were provided based on the established standards. Here is an example:

To ensure compliance with the Medicare *CoPs* you should be reviewing:

- The assessment tool(s) to make sure it is comprehensive, includes all OASIS data, and is completed in the specified time frame

- The initial comprehensive assessment and OASIS data set for inaccuracies

- Primary diagnoses listed on the plan of care and OASIS M0230 to ensure that they are related to the majority of treatments and services listed in the plan of care

- Documentation to ensure that assessments are comprehensive and complete

- Plans of care for completeness, and logical and measurable goals

- That treatments provided are done according to MD orders and documented

- That homebound status is assessed and documented frequently

- Progress notes to make sure they include ongoing and concrete documentation of progress toward goal achievement in a concrete, measurable manner

- Plan of care to ensure that discharge plans and outcomes are documented

- Documented coordination of care among providers and patient

- Documentation of receipt of patient's rights information, required notices, and related information

- Home health aide visit notes to ensure that they reflect the actual service delivered (Zuber, 2004).

Getting your staff to use the audit tool

The audit tool is great for peer-to-peer review. Nurses never like reading their own notes, but when reading someone else's documentation with a tool in hand, the self-realization and peer education flows more readily. Both nurses begin to see the elements that are necessary for complete and accurate nursing documentation. They also begin to see that colleagues struggle with the same issues they do. The approach to the audit process makes it a great way to educate, encourage staff feedback on improving documentation, and celebrate success.

Remember, the audit tool may seem overwhelming at first because it seeks to establish your baseline for meeting the required elements, and therefore is fairly long. But another mantra of yours should be "The bigger the tool, the less you will audit." Let's say your first comprehensive audit tool is three pages long. Although it may seem lengthy, it will help to establish the baseline for the staff's compliance with documentation standards—"testing the water," so to speak. Also, because the audit tool is long, someone will only have to audit two (or whatever number your project team decides) medical records in the time frame established (which should be two weeks). Due to the current decreased lengths of stay, assign a case manager to the clinical record before the 60-day certification period is over. This way, any gaps or problems with the documentation can be resolved before the patient is discharged or the case is closed.

Once a baseline for documentation compliance has been established, share the results with staff. Post them in a simple bar graph. Next, decide which areas most need improvement. Do not take on the entire medical record. Rather, think in terms of high-risk, problem-prone areas. Remember, we all crawled before we walked. Choosing two areas may be all you can accomplish to reach success and sustain it over time.

For example, if you identify documentation of pain assessment and management as needing improvement, you know that this is a critical area of focus for both regulatory and Joint Commission surveyors. With the audit results in hand, you can pull a "rapid action" team together, use a performance improvement process, and set action steps in place to improve the scores.

Advantages of audits for the clinical supervisor

Audits have many advantages for you as a clinical supervisor. They assist you in promoting staff collaboration, increasing compliance in documentation, opening the door for peer-to-peer education, and increasing opportunities for improving staff morale.

Audits also demonstrate your commitment to ongoing PI, which is helpful in defending you against any allegations of negligence related to missing documentation. With the establishment of a firm auditing system, you have demonstrated your commitment to providing quality patient care. You have also demonstrated that you measure the improvements, continue to put in place strategies for improvement, address critical areas quickly, and have set expectations for your staff. In addition:

- You will identify who is not meeting the documentation requirements after counseling, education, and other human resource interventions. This case manager should no longer be a member of your team.

- If an allegation of negligence is filed against you or a member of your staff, you will have a track record of audits, evidence of proactive measures, and an established pattern of good documentation for the nurse(s) involved. In this case, one could argue that one less-than-optimal notation in the medical record does not constitute negligence when the documentation pattern has been stellar in the past.

Finally, the audits will give you an overall picture of any redundancies that exist in the present system. Again, this is a wonderful opportunity to pull a team together to revise the documentation system or simply change the policy. Remember, the goal is to reduce redundancy, meet the required standards, evaluate staff performance, and make the staff happier with the documentation process.

Clinical supervisor tips for auditing

- Use the "KISS" principle—"Keep it simple, silly." The audit tool and its resulting data will need to be understood by several different audiences, so the audit tool and the results must be made comprehensible for everyone.

- Avoid reinventing the wheel. Be sure to use a tool that fits your agency's needs, but seek out an already established audit tool and customize it to meet your requirements.

- Establish a baseline for compliance with the required documentation elements. Use the first comprehensive audit tool and its results to do so.

- Involve staff in the actual auditing of the medical records. To prevent it from becoming an overwhelming task, restrict it to a small sample of clinical records and a short time frame for each auditor.

- Use the results of the audits in your ongoing feedback and annual performance evaluation of the staff nurse. Documentation is a competency that should be part of an employee's job description and performance appraisal.

- Remember to "hold the gains." Audit, audit, and continue to audit.

- Display and celebrate your successes by posting audit results. Always celebrate the successes. Use a run chart, bar graph, or other visual means of showing how well your unit/department is doing.

Sample checklists that can be used to audit medical records can be found in the Appendix.

Resources

Zuber, R. 2004. "Back to the basics: The clinical record." *Home Healthcare Nurse* 22(5):327–332.

Telehealth and electronic health records in home care

Learning objectives

After reading this chapter, the learner will be able to:

- Discuss the advantages and disadvantages of an electronic health record (EHR)
- Identify strategies for a successful transition to an EHR
- Discuss the risk management issues with telehealth in home care

Introduction

Whether or not you want to admit it, the future is already here. For the healthcare industry, it is shortsighted to continue denying that we must integrate technology into our documentation systems. Computers have brought other industries tremendous new successes and efficiencies, and nurses have to change their mindset and get on board—and do it quickly. The home health-care industry has grappled with the use of computers with OASIS data entry and retrieval. But not all systems are created equal. This chapter will discuss realistic expectations and the risks and responsibilities to consider when using technology.

But before we discuss computers and telehealth technology, you need to understand that regardless of the way in which the home care visit is documented it is still the most important step in the home care visit. The case manager may be the only witness to assess the patient's status. In the event of an adverse event or change in condition, documentation will support the nurse in any case of alleged malpractice. Accurate documentation is also needed for appropriate and timely reimbursement. Finally, services are often given by the multidisciplinary team, so good documentation facilitates and demonstrates coordination and continuity of care (Clark, 2003).

Let's recap the elements of the home care visit and how they tie into documentation:

Nursing process	Actions and documentation
Assessment	Review available patient data to determine patient care needs.
Diagnosis	Identify appropriate nursing diagnoses based on available data and assessment.
Planning	• Review previous interventions and outcomes. • Prioritize the patient's needs for your visit. This will help you stay focused on the patient problem and focus your documentation. • Identify and document goals for each visit, preventive interventions.
Implementation	Validate assessment and nursing diagnoses through your documentation. Modify the plan of care as needed.
Evaluation	Evaluate and document the patient's response to your interventions. Identify and document short- and long-term goals.
Document	• Homebound status • Patient assessment and identified health needs • Interventions and patient response to interventions • Outcome of the interventions • Progress toward stated goals on the plan of care • Plan of care for next visit • Patient health status at time of discharge

(Clark, 2003)

How to build a computerized system that reduces liability

There are already systems that can demonstrate benefits to providers and the patient. They allow for the following to occur:

- A physician logs on in his or her office, reviews electronic data, and writes physician orders.

- A home care nurse places a telehealth monitor on the patient, which not only takes the vital signs but also transmits the information and charts it in the medical record.

Easy-to-tote identification cards for migrant workers allow any healthcare provider to access the patient's medical record via the Internet.

- A home care nurse carries a personal digital assistant (PDA) or laptop, in lieu of toting paper clinical records. It provides information at the point of patient care to assist the nurse in identifying when the patient's condition changes.

- Computerized multidisciplinary assessments generate order sets and develop patient care plans that are diagnosis-driven and evidence-based.

- A home care nurse verifies a patient's medication potential for adverse reactions on her laptop.

- Automated audit system allows the clinical supervisor to pinpoint documentation and compliance problems and intervene with specific caregivers.

There is no doubt that the technology for computerized documentation is already fully integrated in our patient-care systems. The challenge for the clinical supervisor will be how to implement strategies that ease the transition for nursing.

Why we need EHRs

Universal access to patient records has become crucial to the delivery of safe and effective healthcare. We saw this during some of our country's worst hours, September 11th and Hurricane Katrina. An integrated nationwide healthcare delivery and information system would have helped many of the sick and injured during these tragedies. In addition, the number of people who need to see healthcare data—such as those in the government, third-party payers, Joint Commission surveyors, and other organizations—continues to grow. The rapid pace of medical and nursing research renders it almost impossible to manage the latest patient-care modalities and the latest technology. Nurses have given this trend of faster, more complicated work the term "complexity compression" (Cummins, 2006). Communication becomes increasingly essential as more patients are seen by multiple healthcare providers. And finally, there is a push for improved patient access and safety through the use of technology.

Consider how much more accurate and available a medication history would be if you had an EHR. Your data analysis and assessments would be more complete and accurate. Care coordination and patient safety would improve, as all of the providers would be able to see the same information at the same time.

Yet there are also disadvantages with electronic records. One major problem is the obvious: when the computers "go down," such as during a power outage or natural disaster. The staff will need a backup system during these events. It also becomes time-consuming, as the data still needs to be entered once the computers are restored. Also, because EHR charting is more structured, the provider is forced to choose form various options in multiple lists—therefore, the author has to change his or her thinking about charting.

Change is difficult, and this change to using technology is no different. Be prepared for resistance. You also need to think about the learning curve of the users and build it into the workload and budget. It may take longer for others to learn the new system of charting, but the need to move forward is here. Documentation on paper or EHR is no different. Also keep in mind that regardless of the software system you choose, there are legal risks also inherent in EHR.

Legal issues in EHR

- You still need to document thoroughly and accurately. Absence of documentation increases your liability for negligence.

- Do not take notes on paper and wait until the end of the day to update the EHR. Timely documentation is just as critical as it is when using a paper system.

- You must protect the privacy of the contents. Do not leave the computer screen open for others to see.

- Technology does not replace clinical judgment. You are still responsible for your actions and documentation.

Whether we agree with the increasing use of computers, we need to be open to the fact that it is here to stay and will be an expectation of all who are in healthcare today and tomorrow. The goal is to have all Americans on an EHR by the year 2014. The push for this agenda is that an EHR facilitates better communication among healthcare providers and patients.

Dr. Brailer of National Health Information Technology identified four goals for the delivery of healthcare:

1. Bring EHRs to point-of-care intersection. This assists providers with real-time information.

2. Provide technology that interconnects with healthcare clinicians.

3. Use this health information technology to give patients more control over health decisions.

4. Use the technology to improve patient care through monitoring, measuring quality and access to evidence-based guidelines (Thompson, 2005).

Start at the beginning

If your organization has decided to invest in a computerized documentation system, the best place to start is at the beginning. If your current documentation system does not work, for example, do not use it as the foundation for the EHR. Rather, start with the old-fashioned approach. Follow the paper trail, from the point of the patient's admission to the point of discharge.

Look at all of the areas the patient encounters, identify everyone who touches the current paper trail, and determine where the paper trail stops to give you an idea of the current gaps in the system. To accomplish these goals, use a workflow chart to help you visualize the current system. Once you have completed the flow chart, ask yourself at every step, "Why are we doing this?" If the answer is "That's the way we have always done it," you have just identified a problem in the system. Your goal is to decrease redundancy and increase efficiency and access to information for better patient outcomes.

Know that there is no such thing as a perfect computerized documentation system. If your existing documentation system has flaws in it, don't approach only the information technology (IT) and health information management (HIM) departments; rather, analyze the flaws and make the necessary changes in the process and the people who use it.

The organization needs to have a clear vision as to what is the patient care model and nursing leadership vision in order for you to set strategic goals for the project and final outcome. Then, you need to find out what all levels of healthcare providers and users—case managers, physical as well as other therapists—need and how they want that information. You likely will find that no one wants to have to go through multiple screens of an EHR to see the whole picture. Providers and users will want to see all of the information pertinent to that patient in a fast, easy format. They want accurate and timely information that will help them manage the patient, decrease the length of stay, and discharge the patient in a more healthy state. Therefore, an interdisciplinary participation is crucial to the end product and the acceptance of the system in the long run.

If your agency is ready to implement an electronic charting system, you should be able to answer the following questions:

- Do we understand that this technology is still relatively new and that there are no government standards currently in place?

- Do we have realistic expectations of the benefits an electronic charting system can provide?

- Are we able to dedicate a full-time employee (FTE) to oversee this project on an ongoing basis—even beyond the start-up?

- Do we have the budget resources available for both the hardware and software needed?

- Is the administration in favor of this change?

- What is the level of the nurses in the use of this technology?

Honest answers to these questions will help you assess your readiness and begin planning for success (DeVore, 2007).

Helpful hints

Appoint a project manager to take the lead in doing the research and making purchase recommendations.

1. Ensure that your agency has reliable Internet access.

2. Review state and federal regulations that may apply.

3. Be sure to do thorough research about what systems are available and within your budget.

4. Include key stakeholders (nurses, therapists, billing staff, etc.) in the decision-making process.

5. Identify specific goals and the benefits your agency expects from the system of choice.

(DeVore, 2007)

Benefits of electronic documentation

Integrating computers into nursing practice will assist your staff in meeting the needs of your patients. It will eliminate the time spent filing, locating, and retrieving patient information. It will also eliminate the issue of illegible handwriting, potentially improving patient safety and reducing liability.

In general, EHRs are seen as the solution to the increased demand for access and analysis of patient information. Carol Langowski looked at five research articles regarding the implementation and satisfaction of online documentation. She found that computerized documentation:

- Allows for fast, real-time access to patient records

- Is efficient, as the information is entered only once

- Has the most current information to help the provider with timely decisions

- Improves quality patient care

- Controls costs with the coordination of information among care providers

- Improves workflow

- Provides red flag alerts when the patient's condition changes

- Improves compliance with regulatory and accreditation agencies when mandatory screens are built into the system

- Helps identify patient acuity and staff productivity (Langowski, 2005)

However, Dr. Trachtenbarg was more realistic in his assessment of the EHRs. Here is his "Myths versus Facts" overview to help you be realistic in the expectations of any EHR system.

Myth	Rationale	Fact
#1 A new EHR system will fix everything	It will not fix organizational problems and does not guarantee improved efficiency and quality. Installing software is just one part of the journey toward improved efficiency and quality.	EHR is not a remedy for all ills. The transition will create problems or have existing problems surface. Be sure your agency will be able to handle the challenges.
#2 Brand A is the best	The correct answer for any EHR software is "It depends."	There is no perfect software. You need to determine what you need the software to do for the agency, improved billing, or documentation.
#3 The software needs to work the way we work	No, maybe the current workflow needs to change to improve outcomes.	An electronic clinical record is not moving from paper to computer. To maximize efficiency the workflow will need to change.
#4 Software will eliminate errors	There is never a substitute for knowledgeable users.	"There is no such thing as an error-proof system."

#5 Discrete data (or structured data entry) is always best	When an EHR system forces the user to document the encounter by choices from a preset list, the data extracted for reporting is better but does not allow for patient variability.	It is best to choose wisely which screens you will use for documentation of discrete data.
#6 Stick to a detailed plan	Actually you can spend too much time planning for the "what ifs."	Best-laid plans may need revision. Be flexible along the way.
#7 You can stop planning	Every system has a finite life cycle.	Be proactive. Start planning for a replacement EHR system. Be sure the vendor has a history of continuous improvement and upgrades.

(Trachtenbarg, 2007)

The clinical supervisor's role

As a clinical supervisor you need to acknowledge one important lesson that has been learned when any organization moves from paper to computerized charting: The process is not automatic. You will need to integrate people, computers, and communication networks (Turpin, 2005). Think about assembling a patient care team that has nursing representation such as yourself, clinical nurse specialists, therapists, and case managers. The role of this team is to review all the patient care processes in place and identify any workflow processes that could be streamlined. In addition, the team will have to standardize protocols ensuring patient quality care and staff compliance and reduce any potential liability (McGurkin, 2006).

When reviewing EHR software, be sure to ask for a demonstration of the system's report-writing capabilities. With these capabilities, a computerized system can help you access patient information far more quickly than you could if you still had to search through the paper documentation system. When reviewing a computerized system, ask yourself the following questions:

- Will there be an improvement in patient care? List the specifics (e.g., improved medication management through the flagging of drug incompatibilities, improved communication among providers).

- Will there be time saved in documentation, data retrieval, preparation of reports, or monitoring quality outcomes?

- Will the information be available when and where it is needed?

- Will it assist the patient providers with decision support?

- Will it be able to organize information specific to the discipline in a manner that is easy to locate?

- Will it eliminate redundancy of patient data?

- Will it provide the patients with evidence-based healthcare?

- Will it provide researchers, reviewers (e.g., state, The Joint Commission), and risk managers with the necessary information?

Challenges associated with change

Let's be honest—no one really likes change. Therefore, the way the agency approaches the transition to an EHR will be pivotal. Remember, you are asking staff members to change how they operate. If they are not good about documenting at the point of care, the transition to an EHR will be difficult. You are asking staff members to change their patterns of documentation, which they may have had for years.

Therefore, it may be difficult to get the nurses to see the value of their documentation. The content of their documentation, as well as the timeliness of the entry, is needed for patient safety and all of the other healthcare team members. If the patient-care information is not up to date, other providers cannot make good clinical decisions. In fact, they may make an error because they can only base their clinical decisions on the information on hand.

Also consider the level of user in the use of the computer. No one likes to feel as if they are less than competent. Computers may be intimidating to some of the staff, so start with a survey to assess the overall competency level. The results will help you identify the amount of education and support you will need in preparation for the go-live day. You will need to plan basic computer training for some of your staff members. After that training, move on to small projects to maintain staff members' ease of use with the computer.

For example, have staff members access the Internet to research issues related to a case study. If they do not have access to computers outside of work, be sure to give them time in the library or computer lab. In addition, if you find someone who is proficient (a "super-user"), use this team member as the shift- and unit-based resource person for the other staff. Your role as the nurse manager will be to continuously monitor staff satisfaction. Your goal is to avoid hostility and negativity within the team, so try to anticipate any resistance that may occur. Use proactive strategies to avert resistance to the new system. You will need to have an understanding of the staff members' perceptions regarding loss of control—the EHR will dictate time frames for their documentation, how they have to document, and what they have to document. These new guidelines may overwhelm and anger some of your staff.

Standardization

There will have to be agreement about both format and transmission standards for data. A successful system does not have different departments with different systems from various vendors that cannot interface. All patient information needs to be shared across all departments.

Security

When introducing the EHR, you will have to address privacy rights (i.e., rights of individuals to decide when, where, and how information about themselves will be shared with others), confidentiality (i.e., protection of patient information from unauthorized use), and protection against data loss. Such security issues will have to be balanced with the nurses' and users' ability to easily access pertinent data. Therefore, you will need policies regarding privacy and security of the EHR.

Your agency will also have to address the use of electronic signatures. Several states have already passed laws legalizing electronic signatures.

These security issues and others should be reviewed by the privacy officer of your facility. Solicit recommendations from your IT manager as well.

Computer etiquette

In this digital age—with a work force that is very comfortable with the use of all forms of digital technology—nurse managers must be on the lookout for proper EHR etiquette. The use of computerized and text communication has become second nature with some of your staff members. This comfort level is reassuring to an extent, as they are less likely to be fearful of any new electronic or digital medium. However, it can become a problem area if staff nurses do not know how to separate informal communication they use for personal interaction with that of professional communication when on duty.

You may find you need a computer etiquette protocol to ensure that the EHR is used in a professional way and to reduce the likelihood of potential litigious actions. Here are a few suggestions to include:

- Use only acceptable abbreviations for all forms of communications
- Be careful about spelling and grammar
- Use polite and courteous language

- Do not use an accusatory or inflammatory tone when communicating with others

- Do not be arrogant

- Do not write anything if you are angry

- Do not breach confidentiality

- Do not write anything you would not want to come back and "bite you"

The dos and don'ts of developing an electronic documentation system
Do

- Have the courage to stick it out, but first be sure you have the right product and the right tools.

- Include the right people in the early stage of development.

- Bring real users on a site visit at other model agencies.

- Ask during a site visit, "How is the support from the vendor?," "How long was the training time?," and "How much resource commitment is necessary?"

- Flow chart the patient's journey through the system. Include and examine every step and ask why the record goes there; consider the challenges at each.

- Ensure that there will be one screen that gives a user the whole picture.

- Include mandatory fields.

- Survey staff computer skills.

- Increase FTEs during the development and training period.

- Ensure that there are sufficient numbers of computers for the users.

- Make the staff use the system over and over again.

- Use table-driven design with drop-down choices. Limit the amount of free text.

- Set expectations that the case managers are to use and document on the computer.

- Identify and use agency-based coaches ("super-users").

- Build a tight security system (e.g., audit trail for each user—who opened the document, when, from what IP address, and using what login name.)

- Develop backup plans for downtime and disaster recovery.

Don't

- Believe that there is one system that can do everything.

- Buy a system that is in beta-testing mode.

- Keep revising as you go along. Set go-live scope requirements and predetermine periodic enhancements.

- Try to duplicate an existing, badly designed paper system.

- Consider buying a system without a site visit.

- Allow for a slow phase-in. Do not let the paper and computer systems straddle each other for too long.

- Let case managers write on paper first.

- Let case managers chart at the end of the visits. It is a bad habit that will have to be broken.

- Allow the patient to feel alienated by the computer user.

- Allow staff to keyboard for someone else.

- Share your frustration about the system with the staff. Keep it to yourself.

Strategies for success

Many organizations around the world have implemented electronic documentation systems. Their successes and failures can be found in the medical, nursing, and IT literature. One of the most comprehensive recommendations can be found in an article by Cecilia Page in *Nursing Economics*. She identified the following factors as critical to success in acceptance of a new clinical information system:

- **Shared vision:** The project must be linked to the organization's strategic plan. The information-management and information systems must follow the financial and operational priorities.

- **Executive leadership:** This is considered the single most critical element of success. The implementation of a clinical documentation system is complex and will affect all clinical disciplines. Therefore, there will need to be a senior leadership sponsor who allocates time for decision-making and arbitration of interdepartmental conflicts. The role of the sponsor will be to ensure success of the clinical information system by helping to overcome any major obstacles.

- **Decision involvement:** Key stakeholders—case managers and other clinicians—will need to be included from the early stages of the process, including the development of the vision. Consider creating a project-advisory committee and a patient-care council, both of which have representatives involved in decisions. Remember that their buy-in will be crucial to the successful implementation of the project.

- **Expectation setting:** As in strategic planning, there should be realistic short-term and long-term goals, with measurable outcomes. Be sure they are clearly communicated to everyone in the organization.

- **Communication process:** Develop a comprehensive communication plan. It should identify target audiences, both internal and external, and frequency of communication. Be creative and use various methods of communication in the plan.

- **Project management:** To ensure success, you will need a project management system, as well as a project manager, with strong project management skills, such as knowing how to plan, execute, control issues, and close the project.

- **Management of system access:** You must conduct a complete evaluation of the environment, including the patient-care delivery system. You will need to be able to answer the following: "Do caregivers on the patient-care unit have ready access to the system? Is the system always available?" Any obstacles to access and availability will sabotage the success of the project.

- **Compatibility of workflow processes:** Before making the switch, your organization will have to streamline the existing documentation system. Nursing documentation should support the nursing process, and the nursing process should reflect patient care in an organized and systematic manner. Evaluate and revise the existing system and then move to automation.

- **Critical mass of data automated:** You will need to integrate the systems that obtain clinical data such as lab values, nursing diagnoses, plan of care, medications, assessment data and related nursing interventions. When clinical data automatically populates the clinical record, clinicians can review and synthesize it.

- **Resource allocation:** The organization will need to ensure budgets for hardware, support systems, replacement staff, and so on. Work with the finance department to ensure that the total costs are factored into not only the first year, but also successive years.

- **System support/administration:** For ongoing success, the organization will need to commit to the appropriate vendor recommendations for system support. There need to be information system support staff who will continue to revise, update, and add to the clinical documentation system. There inevitably will be changes, and for the system to continue to operate smoothly, a designated person will need to make them.

(Page, 2000)

In order for the nursing documentation to be successful in both content and application, you will need to ensure that the EHR incorporates the steps of the nursing process. Doing so will ensure that we, as nurses, complete each step in our role of delivering patient care. Then we need to ensure that the steps can be captured in the EHR.

Legal risks with telehealth in home healthcare

Telehealth devices are becoming more common in the area of home healthcare. It is important for the case managers and the agencies to know the risk-management issues associated with this mode of patient care. According to Hogue, there are two potential types of telehealth liability that you will need to avoid. They are liability for negligence and abandonment.

Liability for negligence applies whenever we care for patients, regardless of the setting. However, when using telehealth devices, the provider as well as the patient must "thoroughly understand how to operate or monitor equipment used to provide telehealth services" (Hogue 2003). To reduce your liability, there needs to be clearly articulated accountability by the device vendor and the agency. This should be described in the written contract with the vendor. The second strategy to avoid liability is to educate the staff and patients about the devices. Claiming that you did not know how to operate a device is no excuse and leads to a claim of negligence. Be sure everyone is trained and deemed competent when using telehealth devices (Hogue, 2003).

The liability for abandonment is not a new legal concept for home health nurses. But home health nurses also need to understand that the liability for abandonment can be attached to this technology as well. A patient could claim that the failure of the device was equal to termination of services from the agency. The following strategies can help to minimize the risk of liability for abandonment when equipment fails or malfunctions:

- Be thorough and realistic in your evaluation of whether the patient is able to care for him or herself in the event of a malfunction or failure.

- If the patient is not capable of caring for him or herself, there must be one primary caregiver able to assist the patient.

- There needs to be continuous assessment of the patient's ability to continue to participate in the telehealth system.

- Confirm the obligations of the patient/caregiver in the event of device malfunction or failure in writing.

(Hogue, 2003)

Remind your staff that technology is simply a tool. It can never replace a nurse at the bedside. Nurses' critical decision-making ability is and will always be vital to quality patient care.

References

Clark, M. 2003. *Community Health Nursing: Caring for Populations,* 4th edition. New Jersey: Pearson.

Cummins, H. J. 2006. "Too much, too fast." *Star Tribune* Minneapolis, MN. December 18, 2006.

DeVore, D. 2007. "Preparing for electronic charting: It's an important first step toward the electronic health record and has to be done right." *Nursing Home Magazine* Jan 2007:28–31.

Hogue, E. 2003. "Telehealth and risk management in home health." *Home Healthcare Nurse* 21(10):699–701.

Langowski, C. 2005. "The times they are a changing: Effects of online nursing documentation systems." *Quality Management in Health Care* 14(2):121–125.

McGurkin, T. 2006. "IT takes a care team." *Nursing Management* 37(3):18–20, 23, 31.

Page, C. 2000. "Critical success factors for implementing a clinical information system." *Nursing Economics* 18(5):255–256.

Thompson, B. 2005. "The transforming effect of handheld computers on nursing practice." *Nursing Administration Quarterly* 29(4):308–314.

Trachtenbarg, D. 2007. "EHRs fix everything—and nine other myths." *Family Practice Management* Mar:26–30.

Turpin, P. 2005. "Transitioning from paper to computerized documentation" *Gastroenterology Nursing* 28(1):61–62.

Motivating yourself and others to document completely and accurately

Learning objectives

After reading this chapter, the learner will be able to:

- Discuss why nursing staff members have difficulty complying with nursing documentation standards
- Identify motivational strategies to increase compliance with clinical record documentation

Why nurses document poorly

To make the necessary changes to anyone's documentation habits, you will need to understand the why and the how behind what they do.

You must first figure out why you are not documenting to your agency's expectations. Ask yourself: Do I really document well enough to avoid legal risks? Then, you must determine how to change these attitudes and behaviors. Regardless of the setting, understanding what impedes and motivates nurses and their documentation will be essential in improving documentation.

Documentation issues are universal. They occur in all areas of healthcare and in all countries. In 2003, a postgraduate research student studied the reasons for poor documentation and published the results in the *British Journal of Nursing*. Some of the reasons were:

- Nurses' apathy about documentation
- The time-consuming nature of documentation
- Discrepancies between nurse-patient and nurse-nurse interpretation of the significance of the event
- Nurses' literacy skills

Darmer reported on results from Denmark regarding nurses' knowledge and attitudes toward documentation and how to improve nursing documentation in anticipation of computerized documentation systems. The recommendations were that organizations need structured intervention programs to improve the quality of nursing documentation. The study also recommended:

- Training the entire staff simultaneously versus using key persons as peer trainers

- Clinical supervision and chart audits to increase learning on the supervisory and staff levels

- Support of hospital management

- Nurse managers need to be proficient in nursing theories and practice (Darmer, 2006)

Another nursing research study looked at the complexities of nursing documentation. This study found that initial assessments are commonly incomplete. Most nursing records have no nursing diagnoses and those identified are physical in nature with few psychosocial needs identified. When nursing interventions are recorded, they do not take into account the patient's view at that time. Some of the problems the study identified were:

- Nurses' notes were written in a repetitive manner or excluded meaningful data

- Numerous documentation forms and an inconvenient system produce data redundancy

- Some formats were too long, repetitious, and time-consuming

- Forms that were used did not capture the amount of nursing care provided

- Descriptive-style documentation systems are no longer appropriate for the current workload or responsibilities of clinical nurses (Cheevakasemsook, 2006)

It is clear that although there are obvious legal and professional benefits of good nursing documentation, nurses' attitudes toward it will not change unless we effectively convey its value.

Many nurses resent the amount of documentation they are required to do and feel that it takes them away from patient care. Given this longstanding attitude, any good agency will make its documentation system more concise and focused—and evaluate it as a top priority. Nurses need to understand that documentation is an inherent part of nursing and not a distinct practice from it.

In addition to resistance from nurses, organizational problems may affect the quality of nursing documentation. Look within your organization. Is there a lack of consistency in documentation between nurses? For example, is important and pertinent information recorded in an inappropriate place, such as care coordination notes versus visit or progress notes? Such inconsistency can lead to patient care being compromised, omitted, or replicated.

Another issue may be a language barrier. Nurses whose first language is not English may have difficulty interpreting speech, nursing documentation forms, and progress notes. They may lack the necessary skills to make an adequate written record of their observations, and they may have difficulty interpreting other staff nurses' documentation. Therefore, if you have staff members who are not comfortable with the English language, you need to review their documentation on a regular basis. Additional education and language resources may be needed to improve the accuracy of the patient record and the overall safety of the patients in your agency.

If you are a clinical supervisor, your role is to understand the barriers to improving nursing documentation and develop strategies you can use to achieve the goal of quality documentation.

"This is the Age of Instability, where managing change is everybody's job. Think of it as your personal assignment." —Prichett and Pound

Change: Embrace it or resist it

As a clinical supervisor or case manager, you must ask yourself how you feel about change. Change was the universal language of the '90s, and it will continue to be the universal language now and in the future. It is unavoidable. The world is changing, and our healthcare environment is constantly changing as well.

Often, we fear change because it disrupts the way we see ourselves, our familiar rituals, and routines. Woodrow Wilson said, "If you want to make enemies, try to change something." It will be a challenge to ask your staff members to change the way they document to meet new standards or change from a paper-based to a computerized documentation system. Before any changes, everyone needs to evaluate their attitudes about change and their ability to manage it.

If you have admitted that you do not like change, then take small steps toward accepting it more readily. Start with taking a different route to work tomorrow. Spend your lunch hour in a totally new way. Plan to do something this weekend you have never done before. Volunteer to do something you normally would not do. Every day this week, say, "Why not?" to someone who says that something cannot be done.

If you need a quick reference for change—and one that everyone can relate to—read the bestselling book *Who Moved My Cheese?* by Spencer Johnson. He helps us identify which type of person we are in terms of our attitude toward change, whether it be in our work or professional life.

"Example is not the main thing in influencing others: It's the only thing."—*Albert Schweitzer*

Sullivan (2005) says that nurses in management positions need to be prepared for resistance from the staff when they hear the following:

- "We tried that before."

- "No one else does it like that."

- "We've always done it this way."

- "We don't have the time."

Do you know how you will handle resisters? Prepare yourself by expecting some resistance to change. Listen to the staff carefully—who is saying what, when, in what circumstances? Be alert for nonverbal signs of resistance, such as poor work habits or lack of interest in the change. It will be your job to know the change inside and out, as you will have to defend it against any challengers. Remember not to personalize the resistance; learn to minimize it.

Here are some guidelines in managing change:

- Always communicate with anyone who opposes the change. Find out why they are opposed to the change.

- Clarify any information and give accurate feedback.

- Be open to suggestions and revisions, but be clear about what is not negotiable.

- Present the consequences of resistance as it pertains to the organization's survival or compromised patient care.

- Always point out the positive consequences of the change.

- Use your supporters—those shining stars on your unit—to have face-to-face contact with resisters.

- Demonstrate your support and confidence in the staff and the change process. (Sullivan, 2005).

The role of education and expectations

To motivate staff for any necessary change, start with orientation. All staff should know what the expectations are as a team member. It is important that everyone be informed of the mission, values, and vision for the organization. Include some of the successful changes that the organization has achieved in the past few years. This gives everyone a sense that change is important and achievable at your organization.

In relation to documentation, review the job description and highlight the key job elements that will be needed to demonstrate competency, as well as for the annual performance evaluation. Just as audits are an important aspect of successful documentation outcomes, so too are ongoing education sessions. And always include case study examples during the education sessions, as they will be more meaningful to the staff.

Nursing documentation needs to have the same level of attention and commitment to quality maintenance as annual competencies. Therefore, use audit results, case reviews, and mandatory documentation education as motivation tools. The best motivator, however, is giving the staff feedback. The feedback could be positive or negative—staff response will depend entirely on the way it is handled.

Work should be a nice, stress-free environment. Use various ways to showcase documentation issues or successes. Be creative in how you post clinical documentation outcomes and quality improvement reports. In an earlier chapter, we discussed how to get the staff involved. Peer-to-peer participation in the audit process is a valuable tool for improving teamwork, professional growth, and self-awareness. The performance appraisal should also be used, as key job elements usually specify the use of the nursing process and how it is evaluated based on the documentation of patient care.

When someone is reviewing a case, for example, give the involved staff timely feedback on what was found or not found in the clinical record. And always remind the record reviewer to point out the positive and negative aspects of what was found. This method is one of the most effective because the staff members receive feedback at the time of the review, which makes them more likely to remember and not repeat the mistake in another clinical record.

Education is not a standalone cure. It needs to be supported by setting expectations and achievable goals and coaching as part of the reinforcement.

For example, if the agency changes to an electronic documentation system, your role as a clinical supervisor is to observe staff and give positive feedback on how well they use the new system. If you have a staff member who is struggling with it, your job is to identify ways to assist this staff member. It may require more education, time practicing computer skills, or time with the agency's "super-user." Remember, success will be based on how well you manage your staff through this new process.

The good, the bad, and the ugly approach

The following approach to meeting your nursing documentation goals is my favorite. Set up a designated area for posting "the good, the bad, and the ugly." Or, if you have a monthly staff meeting or newsletter, include this method of feedback. As part of ongoing feedback, use case studies to demonstrate good documentation, bad (improper) documentation, and really ugly (potential for liability) documentation as a motivator. You must remember to maintain patient and staff-member anonymity by blacking out the patient identifiers and the author's signature.

For examples of good documentation, pay attention during the chart audit process. Look for a nurse or other licensed professional who uses good documentation skills and follows the agency's protocol in documentation. Ask the author of the documentation for permission to post this sample so others can learn from it.

Next choose examples of "the bad." Find an example of a nurse who did not include the critical aspects of documentation, or find an example of someone who failed to follow the agency's policy or protocol. Post these examples in the appropriate section next to the good example. The purpose of the bad example is to demonstrate that the author missed critical documentation aspects such as date, time, and evidence of the nursing process and critical thinking. There could be gaps in documentation or omissions of information that should have been entered.

The "ugly" example is the one that violates several aspects of good documentation. It could show the author using unacceptable abbreviations (which is a violation of a Joint Commission National Patient Safety Goal), illegible handwriting, "finger pointing," or no follow-through—any improper documentation that could lead to lack of reimbursement by payers or allegations of negligence.

"The art of progress is to preserve order amid change and to preserve change amid order."
—*Alfred North Whitehead*

Monitoring the work environment

Staff will need your leadership during any period of change. To lessen the feelings of loss of control, you must ensure a positive work environment. You will also need to control the other processes (e.g., adequate supplies) that, although not affected by the documentation changes, will impact the work day for staff.

To ease the change further, provide staff with interesting work, a fun environment, and as much positive feedback as possible. The role of humor cannot be underestimated. During stressful times, laughing at oneself or at the process of change can do wonders—provided the humor is not at the expense of someone's feelings. Start a humor board, for example. Staff can bring in cartoons, one-liners, etc., concerning the change or topic of the month. Or consider a quote-of-the-day humor board. Everyone needs a smile at least once a day.

In addition to humor, teamwork will be essential to achieving your goal. It is your responsibility to ensure that staff members have good relationships with everyone on the team. You will need to intervene if there are members of the team who undermine the process or refuse to work toward team goals. There are shining stars and resisters in every work environment, and you already know who they are. You must now use them to assist you in making the necessary changes to the new documentation system. Here is an example of what has worked successfully in the past:

Take your shining stars, your informal leaders, and your resisters, and put them all on the same project team (in both the development and auditing stages). Your role will be to facilitate the project team to work to their identified goal. The shining stars are to coach the remaining staff on why and how the change is possible. The informal leaders will need to be convinced that the change is good and possible. They work undercover, so you must monitor what is being said outside of the team meetings.

The resisters are put on the team as a way to educate them about the needed change and encourage them to become part of the change. Resisters may need one-on-one work with you if they begin to sabotage the process. When you sense or hear griping, turn it into a positive with the exercise in Figure 10.1.

| Figure 10.1 | Transforming a gripe into a goal in five minutes |

1. Begin by identifying a situation in your work life that you consider to be a problem.
My frustration, gripe, or difficulty is that _____
_____
_____

2. Elaborate on this problem in one sentence that begins with the words:
My real concern is _____
_____
_____

3. Behind almost every concern, there lies a wish. Take the concern you have just identified, turn it upside down, and write one sentence that begins with the words:
What I am really wishing for is _____
_____
_____

4. Keeping in mind all of the above and everything else you know about this problem, finish the following sentence:
Therefore, my goal is to _____
_____

(Your goal may be identical to your wish. If your wish is too idealistic or impractical, write down what you would settle for.)

5. Finally, write in the word "How" between the words "is" and "to" in step 4 above:
My goal (problem) is how to _____
_____
_____

You have now clearly defined your problem, enabling you to communicate it to others in such a way that they will be able to help you.

Use this exercise:

- For yourself, when you are frustrated with a problem and cannot get a handle on how to solve it

- If you want someone's help in solving a problem

- When you hear someone expressing frustration about a current situation

- Whenever a group meeting begins to turn into a gripe session

Be sure to show staff members that the organization is loyal to them. Encourage administration to stop in and ask staff members how they are doing. Remember that even small gestures of appreciation go a long way. Make sure your project has a plan for small, intermittent "celebrations" (e.g., bake-offs, pizza parties, raffles) to keep up the energy level of the staff. The key here is to keep celebrations small and include everyone. Remember that no change will be implemented without staff involvement. Continuously monitor your staff for reaction and intervene whenever necessary to set them back on course.

"Our moral responsibility is not to stop the future, but to shape it . . . to channel our destiny in humane directions and to ease the trauma of transition."—Alvin Toffler, American futurist

Tips

Staff-motivation tips for clinical supervisors

- Make your presence known. Show staff members that you are a leader.
- Constantly search for new ideas. Involve mentors, colleagues, and staff.
- Trust your staff members and empower them; they will not let you down.
- Use the GOYA (Get Out of Your Armchair) approach. In other words, once the captain has set the course, he or she has to walk around and find out how the ship is running.
- Strive for constant improvement. Everyone wants to work on a winning team.
- Set your clear expectations for the staff, and they will rise to the level of your expectations.
- Always be honest. Tell them the good with the bad.
- Never back off from your goals.
- Do not be afraid to take risks. It is better to ask for forgiveness than to ask for permission.
- Listen—really listen.
- Don't even think of asking your staff to change if you have no intention of changing.
- Always change yourself first.

References

Cheevakasemsook, A. 2006. "The study of nursing documentation complexities." *International Journal of Nursing Practice* 12(6):366–374.

Darmer, M. 2006. "Nursing documentation audit: The effect of a VIPS implementation programme in Denmark." *Journal of Clinical Nursing* 15(5):525–534.

Johnson, S. 1998. *Who Moved My Cheese?* New York: GP Putnam's Sons.

Prichett, P. 1992. *The Employee Handbook for Organizational Change.* Dallas: Prichett Publishing.

Sullivan, E. 2005. *Effective Leadership and Management in Nursing.* Upper Saddle River, New Jersey: Pearson Prentice Hall.

Taylor, H. 2003. "An exploration of the factors that affect nurses' record keeping." *British Journal of Nursing* 12(12):751–758.

Appendix

OBQI CLINICAL RECORD REVIEW

ADVERSE EVENT:
EMERGENT CARE FOR INJURY CAUSED BY FALL OR ACCIDENT

Quarter/Year: _____   Reviewer: _____

Case Manager: _____   Patient: _____

ID Number: _____   SOC: _____   D/C: _____

Responses extracted from record	Reviewer Notes
M0230 Primary Diagnosis (ICD-9/Descriptor) 1.)	
M0240 Other diagnoses (ICD-9/Descriptor) 2.) 3.)	
Date/Time of Injury	
Nature of Injury: ☐ Dislocation/Fx ☐ Contusion/Laceration ☐ Concussion ☐ Other:	
Follow-Up Action: ☐ ED Eval and Release ☐ Admitted for 23 hours ☐ Acute Care Admission ☐ Other:	

Safety Risk Potential Rating:	Yes	No	N/A	Reviewer Notes
Safety Assessment is completed at SOC				
Safety instruction is incorporated into the POC on the 485				
Energy conservation instruction is incorporated into the POC on the 485				
Patient teaching and response is evidenced				
Barriers to teaching/learning are evidenced				
Patient Event Report was completed				
Practitioner present at time of incident				

OASIS ITEM	RISK MARKER	YES	NO	UK
M0066 Age	Over 65			
M0230/240 Diagnosis/Severity Index	More than one Chronic Illness			
M0310 Structural Barrieres	1 – 4			
M0320 Safety Hazards	1 – 9			
M0330 Sanitation Hazards	3, 4, 9, 11			
M0390 Vision	1 – 2			
M0520 Urinary Incontinence	1 – 2			
M0560 Cognitive Functioning	2 – 4			
M0570 When Confused	2 – 4			
M0650 Dress Upper Body	2 – 3			
M0660 Dress Lower Body	2 – 3			
M0670 Bathing	3 – 5			
M0680 Toileting	2 – 4			
M0690 Transferring	2 – 5			
M0700 Ambulation	1 – 5			
M0780 Management of Medications	1 – 2			
OASIS ITEM	RISK MARKER	YES	NO	UK
M0420 Pain	2 - 3			
M0490 Dyspnea	2 - 4			
M0500 Oxygen	1 - 4			
MEDICATIONS	RISK MARKER			
Psychotropic Drugs				
Noncompliance				
	TOTAL			

Patient is at risk for falls with any "Yes" response.

Using the following scale, indicate the patient's risk

Based on number of "Yes" answers.

Low < I___I___I___I___I___I___I > High

0   3   6   9   12   15   18

A-1

Conclusion:
- ☐ **No Adverse Event Outcome**
- ☐ **Adverse Event not related to care**
- ☐ **OASIS data integrity error**
- ☐ **Quality Concern**
- ☐ **Technical Concern**

OTHER FINDINGS:

_____
_____
_____
_____
_____
_____
_____
_____
_____
_____
_____
_____
_____
_____
_____

Practitioner Comments:

Practitioner Signature: _____ Date: _____

Source: St. Peter's Health Care Services—Home Care Department.

DOCUMENTATION AUDIT TOOL

Practitioner: _____ Patient Initials: _____ SOC Date: _____

Reviewer: _____ Date of Review: _____

Indicator	Yes	No	N/A	Comments
Does the CMS-485 reflect the problems identified in the initial OASIS assessment?				
Are the OASIS items consistent with documented visit narratives?				
Is the SOC OASIS completed within 24 hours?				
Is there an OASIS assessment for every occurrence: SOC, transfer, ROC, Follow-Up, D/C?				
Was the POC reviewed with the MD at the SOC?				
Was MD notified of changes to the POC or change in patient status?				
Are all meds the patient is taking at the SOC, including over-the-counter, listed on the CMS-485 with route, dose, and frequency?				
Is the medication profile updated with additions/changes?				
Is immunization status assessed and documented?				
Are there orders for all disciplines involved?				
If therapy is ordered, is there a therapy-related diagnosis on the 485?				
Is there coordination of care between disciplines?				
Are there interim orders for any changes to the POC?				
Were visits made at the ordered frequency?				
Is there documentation of progress or lack of progress toward goals?				
Is the content of instructions given and the patient/caregiver's response to teaching noted?				
Is there evidence of discharge planning with the patient?				
Does each note reflect skilled care being performed?				
Does each note stand alone?				
Is there a finite and realistic date for qd or bid visits?				
Are there weekly wound measurements?				

A-2

Do wound measurements include three dimensions (LxWxD)?				
Are wounds measured in centimeters?				
Has there been an WOCN consult for bid or qd wounds?				
Orders are present for all treatments being performed?				
Are all medications administered by staff charted to include the med, time, route, dose, effects and absence of adverse reaction?				
Do notes contain only SPHHC approved abbreviations?				
Are HHA supervisions performed every 14 days or less?				
Are revisit notes completed within 24 hours and locked?				
Are the patient's stated pain goals documented?				
Is edema documented per standard (1+ etc. for pitting; centimeters for non-pitting)?				
Was D/C OASIS completed within 48 hours of D/C date?				

OTHER FINDINGS/COMMENTS:

Practitioner Comments:

Practitioner Signature: _____ Date: _____

90 – 100% earns a factor of 1
80 – 89% earns a factor of .95
70 – 79% earns a factor of .85 Points
Less than 70% earns a factor of .85

EXAMPLE:

Job Performance Appraisal Score	Documentation Factor	Earned
120 Points	1	120 Points
120 Points	.95	114 Points
120 Points	.90	108 Points
120 Points	.85	102 Points

W:H\Shared\Forms(DocumentationAuditTool2007.doc)1/07

Source: St. Peter's Health Care Services—Home Care Department.

A-3

OBQI CLINICAL RECORD REVIEW
ADVERSE EVENT :
EMERGENT CARE FOR HYPO/HYPERGLYCEMIA

Quarter/Year: _____   Reviewer: _____

Case Manager: _____   Team: _____

Patient: _____   ID Number: _____

SOC: _____   D/C: _____

Responses extracted from record	Reviewer Notes
M0230 Primary Diagnosis (ICD-9/Descriptor) 1.)	
M0240 Other Diagnoses (ICD-9/Descriptor) 2.) 3.)	
M0780/790 Management of Oral/Injectable Medications SOC: ☐ Take independently ☐ Take with Assist ☐ Unable ☐ N/A D/C: ☐ Take independently ☐ Take with Assist ☐ Unable ☐ N/A	
Date of Occurrence/Circumstance	
Follow-Up Action: ☐ ED Eval and Release ☐ Admitted for 23 hours ☐ Acute Care Admission ☐ Other:	
Number of Medications Patient is currently taking	
SOC OASIS and D/C OASIS completed by same practitioner	
Physical findings that might contribute to emergent care: Cognitive deficit, change in mental status, loss of caregiver assistance, decline in functional status, noncompliance.	

	YES	NO	N/A	
Is Endocrine Status Assessment incorporated in 485				
Is Diabetic instruction incorporated into Original POC on 485.				
Communication with MD re: relevant change in patient's status is evidenced				
Orders are present for changes in medication				
Medication profile is updated with changes				
Patient teaching and response specific to medication administration is evidenced				
Barriers to teaching/learning are documented				

ADVERSE EVENT :
EMERGENT CARE FOR HYPO/HYPERGLYCEMIA

Conclusion:
☐   **No Adverse Event Outcome**
☐   **Adverse Event not related to care**
☐   **OASIS data integrity error**
☐   **Quality Concern**

A-3

☐   **Technical Concern**

OTHER FINDINGS:

_____
_____
_____
_____
_____
_____
_____
_____
_____
_____
_____
_____
_____
_____

Practitioner Comments:

Practitioner Signature: _____   Date: _____

Source: St. Peter's Health Care Services—Home Care Department.

A-4

OBQI CLINICAL RECORD REVIEW

__ADVERSE EVENT :__
__EMERGENT CARE FOR WOUND INFECTION, DETERIORATING WOUND STATUS__

Quarter/Year: _____   Reviewer: _____

Case Manager: _____   Team: _____

Patient: _____   ID Number: _____

SOC: _____   D/C: _____

Responses extracted from record	Reviewer Notes
M0230 Primary Diagnosis (ICD-9/Descriptor) 1.)	
M0240 Other Diagnoses (ICD-9/Descriptor) 2.) 3.)	
Integumentary Assessment appropriately completed ☐ Yes ☐ No	
M0488: Status of most Problematic Wound SOC: ☐ Full.Gran. ☐ Early Granulating ☐ Not Healing ☐ N/A D/C: ☐ Full Gran. ☐ Early Granulating ☐ Not Healing ☐ N/A	
Wound Care is performed by: ☐ RN ☐ Pt/Caregiver ☐ Both	
Date of Occurrence/Circumstance	
Follow-Up Action: ☐ ED Eval and Release ☐ Admitted for 23 hours ☐ Acute Care Admission ☐ Other:	
SOC OASIS and D/C OASIS completed by same practitioner	

	YES	NO	N/A	Reviewer Notes
POC is being followed regarding Assessment/Interventions/Instructions				
Communication with MD re: relevant change in patient's status is evidenced				
Orders are present for changes in treatment				
Nutritional interventions are incorporated into POC if screened at risk				
Wound Care is measured per standard				
Consult with enterostomal RN is initiated for difficult wounds and/or if no healing in 3 weeks				
Patient teaching and response specific to wound care is evidenced				

__ADVERSE EVENT :__
__EMERGENT CARE FOR WOUND INFECTION, DETERIORATING WOUND STATUS__

	YES	NO	N/A	Reviewer Notes
Barriers to teaching/learning are documented				
Consistency of staff is evidenced				

A-4

Conclusion:
☐　　No Adverse Event Outcome
☐　　Adverse Event not related to care
☐　　OASIS data integrity error
☐　　Quality Concern
☐　　Technical Concern

OTHER FINDINGS:

Practitioner Comments:

Practitioner Signature: _____　Date: _____

Source: St. Peter's Health Care Services—Home Care Department.

A-5

ZIP CHECK HOME HEALTH FUNCTIONAL ASSESSMENT
(Module A)
Survey date: _____
Pt initials: _____ **Age:** _____ **Sex:** M F   **SOC Date:** _____
A12. **Principal Dx:** _____ A13. **Surgical Dx:** _____ A14. **Other Dx:** _____
A15. **Impairments:** Speech Hearing Vision None
A16. **Medication Orders** (check for notation in record)
_____ Contraindications _____ Psychotropic/mood altering drugs _____ Other:
_____ HHA awareness of drug sensitivity/allergies; visible warnings on pt record

A19. Review POC and interim orders for type, duration, and freq of services (calendar worksheet)
    Y   N   Were services delivered as ordered ?
A20. Anticipated pt outcomes R/T medical, nsg, and rehab services. Pt and condition specific outcomes
should be measurable and quantifiable. Include date outcome was defined and/or revised.
Level of Achievement for Pt Care Outcomes

	Complete	Partially	Not at All	Comments
1.				
2.				
3.				
4.				
5.				
6.				

> 6 outcomes? **Y N** (Cont on back) Is there evidence of planning toward discharge? **Y N Not appropriate**	Does record contain progress notes that describe the level of achievement for anticipated outcomes? **Y Some N**

Auditor Notes:
_____
_____
_____
_____

B. 6 Surveyor Note: If needs assistance with ADLs-Does Medical record document planning to provide
additional help?

A-5

HHA REVIEW AREA (Module D)

Documentation Record completeness	Substantially Complete	Partially Complete	Substantially Incomplete		Surveyor Notes:
Documentation Record agrees w/ in-home observation	**Substantially**	**Partially**	**Not at All**		
HHA Adherence to Plan Medical condition ADL	**Complete Adherence**	**Partial Adherence**	**No Adherence**	Check here if no ADL POC ☐	
Pt Cond (relative to cond at adm) Medical condition ADL	**Improved**	**Unchanged**	**Deteriorated**	Check here if ADL status and treatment are not relevant to this case. ☐	

SUMMARY OF EVAL OF PT'S CARE	Explain No's
D2. Were HHA assessments of the pt's medical, nsg and rehab needs appropriate at the SOC and as the care progressed? Y N	
D3. Were the types and freq of services prescribed in the initial POC appropriate, given the pt's anticipated outcomes and cond (s) at adm? Y N	
D4. Did you see evidence that the pt's POC was changed appropriately during the course of care to reflect any changes in medical, nsg and rehab needs? **No change required** Y N	
D5. Did you see evidence of coord of services between and among the disciplines treating this pt? **N/A only one discipline** Y N	
D6. Did orders for therapy services include the specific procedures and modalities to be used, as well as the amt, freq, and duration of services? **N/A no therapy services ordered** Y N	
D7. Did you home visit lead you to conclude that the pt's progress (or lack of progress), was appropriate given the pt's admitting and current medical and functional status? Y N	
D8. Does the evidence from your review of the record, your conversation with HHA nurse and your home visit lead you to conclude that the HHA intervened appropriately, and made a difference in the pt's current medical and functional capacity? Y N	
D9. In your opinion, could the HHA have done more to assist this pt in meeting his/her medical, nsg, rehab needs w/in the range of usual HHA practice? If yes, record specific examples. Y N	

A-6

DOCUMENTATION TIPS ON MEDICAL NECCESITY, QUALITY AND REIMBURSEMENT

DOCUMENT . . .	CV	RESP	HEP/PANC	SKIN	MUS	NEURO	GU	PSY	ONCOLOGY	HOSPICE	ANTE-PARTAL
Specific care provided, including response to care and plan for next visit	X	X	X	X	X	X	X	X	X	X	X
Congruency between visit notes and OASIS	X	X	X	X	X	X	X	X	X	X	
Specific reason for homebound status in functional terms	X	X	X	X	X	X	X	X	X	X	
Lab and other objective findings: "tell the story" of progress toward goal achievement	X	X	X	X	X	X	X	X	X	X	
Any identified barriers to learning	X	X	X	X	X	X	X	X	X	X	
Care coordination (MD, team members, pt/caregiver)	X	X	X	X	X	X	X	X	X	X	
Change in the patient's condition, if applicable	X	X	X	X	X	X	X	X	X		
Objective, measurable information to support skilled care and need for nursing intervention	X	X	X	X	X	X	X	X	X		
Any variance to the goals/outcomes	X	X	X	X	X	X	X	X	X		X
All communication (phone calls, team meetings, etc.)	X	X	X	X	X	X	X	X	X		
All supplies required even if not part of the skilled service needs	X	X									
Emergency preparedness whether it be patient, caregiver, neighbor, friend		X	X		X	X	X			X	
O2 orders on medication list		X									
Oximetry results		X									
Support for therapy services if patient is receiving PT, OT, SLT	X								X		
Realistic and projected endpoint (specific date) if you are providing care seven days/week			X		X		X		X		
Pain using characteristic, location, duration, onset, intensity, etc.			X		X	X	X		Xper		
PRN visit orders for Foley complication necessitating a home visit for assessment (e.g., dysuria, hematuria, dislodgement, catheter falls out)							X				
PRN visit orders for ileal conduit care and management of appliances and skin							X				
Specific supplies used on 485 and obtain specific orders			X	X	X		X			X	
Wound care supplies including those used in the care and prevention of infection				X							

DOCUMENT . . .	CV	RESP	HEP/PANC	SKIN	MUS	NEURO	GU	PSY	ONCOLOGY	HOS-PICE	ANTE-PARTAL
Progress towards wound healing; measure at least once/week or per agency protocol; include location, size, drainage, color, amount and care				X							

A-6

DOCUMENT . . .	CV	RESP	HEP/PANC	SKIN	MUS	NEURO	GU	PSY	ONCOLOGY	HOS-PICE	ANTE-PARTAL
provided											
Patient or wound deterioration				X							
Any change that impacts provision of safe care				X							
Specific teaching conducted-to whom and behavioral outcomes of that teaching				X							X
Wound drainage, amount and site, etc.; if cultured the results				X							
Any medication changes to the POC; or medication- related side effects				X		X			X		
Level of patient's participation in care				X							
Any communication in POC changes				X	X	X			X		X
Photographs taken at onset and every 3 weeks; patient must sign release; place photo in clinical record				X	X	X					
If patient/family member unable to do dressing (e.g., retinopathy, location of wound, family only able to provide evening care, severity of wound, etc.)				X							
The need for 10+ therapy assessment visits (places patient into a heavier weighted higher-reimbursed HHRG)					X						
Specific functional limits					X						
Patient's many skilled needs: observation and assessment; teaching and training; hands-on skilled care (e.g., feeding tube, bowel and bladder, suctioning)					X						
Any additional orders for service, treatment or care not on the original POC					X						
Specific skill proved as clearly as possible					X						
Need for HHA due to the inability of patient to do ADLs, personal hygiene					X						
Progress toward predetermined, patient-centered goals					X						
Seizure or other problematic neurologic activity					X						

DOCUMENT . . .	CV	RESP	HEP/PANC	SKIN	MUS	NEURO	GU	PSY	ONCOLOGY	HOS-PICE	ANTE-PARTAL
Skilled "hands on" nursing care; professional support and case management, wound care, medication administration, observation and assessment, pain management									X		
Any abnormal BP findings, blood results and/or protein in urine											X

A-6

Uncontrolled HTN, anemia necessitating EPO injections, dsg changes for abdominal sites, neurovascular ulcer sites or wound care, medication management, CVA, poorly controlled DM	X	
Nursing visits to administer epoetin injections	X	
Any problems related to patient and cath care (e.g., constipation, pressure on the bladder, need for different size or type of cath, bladder spasms, increased or changed sediment, leaking)	X	

Adapted from Marrelli, T 2001. *Handbook of Home Health Standards and Documentation Guidelines for Reimbursement*